Acclaim for
God Is Greater Than . . . Family Mess

"My friend Joey Johnson has done all of us a great favor! Read this book for a fresh grip on a great home and a compelling glimpse of a great God."

—Joseph Stowell, President Moody Bible Institute

"Joey Johnson is a leader whose pastoral vision is wise and compassionate, whose leadership is prophetic and biblically centered, whose passion is for a Spirit-filled, Christ-exalting Church, and whose integrity is pure and proven. I commend his ministry as well as his new book, *God Is Greater Than . . . Family Mess.*"

—Jack W. Hayford, Litt.D.
Pastor/Chancellor
The Church On The Way
The King's Seminary
Van Nuys, California

"There are some books that are written just to be written and others that ought to be written but never are, but this book had to be written and thank God it has been. With the skill of a scholar, the passion of a preacher and the profundity and perspective of a pastor, Joey Johnson has exposed and revealed the *Family Mess* that so many live with, struggle with and seek to hide and avoid. This book speaks to where we are and how we live, but will not let us be content to stay there. Pastor Joey assures us that God can turn the mess into a miracle. Read this book and be blessed, read it and be helped, read it and be changed."

—Bishop Timothy J. Cl~
First Church ~
City of
Columbu~

Acclaim for
God Is Greater Than . . . Family Mess

"Journey with Joey Johnson through the family histories of the Bible to discover your own family history today."

—Leith Anderson
President
National Associate of Evangelicals
Washington, D.C.

"With the abundance of books published on the topic of family, it would seem to be next to impossible to say anything fresh or innovative. Pastor Johnson has accomplished the 'next to impossible.' Not only is his insight into family life and family dysfunction fresh, it is also thoroughly biblical. You'll never read the book of Genesis the same way again. This is a very welcome and much needed addition to Christian literature on the family."

—Rich Nathan
Senior Pastor
Vineyard Columbus

GOD IS GREATER THAN...

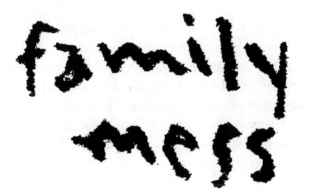

family mess

GOD IS GREATER THAN...

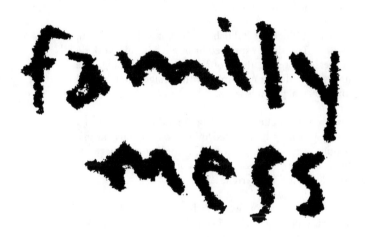

family mess

PASTOR JOEY JOHNSON

WINEPRESS WP PUBLISHING

Packaged by WinePress Publishing, PO Box 428, Enumclaw, WA 98022. The views expressed or implied in this work do not necessarily reflect those of WinePress Publishing. The author is ultimately responsible for the design, content, and editorial accuracy of this work.

Front Cover Design and Title Graphic by Betro Communications, Inc. 330.945.9836 betroinc@earthlink.net.

Unless otherwise noted, all Scriptures are taken from the New American Standard Bible, © 1960, 1963, 1968, 1971, 1972, 1973, 1975, 1977 by The Lockman Foundation. Used by permission.

Scriptures marked NIV are taken from the Holy Bible, New International Version, Copyright © 1973, 1978, 1984 by the International Bible Society. Used by permission of Zondervan Publishing House. The "NIV" and "New International Version" trademarks are registered in the United States Patent and Trademark Office by International Bible Society.

Scriptures marked KJV are taken from the King James Version of the Bible.

ISBN 1-57921-426-6
Library of Congress Catalog Card Number: 2001097133

Acknowledgements

I want to thank and give honor to my God, who has used me in spite of my sins because He has an eternal destiny for me.

Special thanks to my wife, Cathy, for her long years of support and encouragement in an exciting, growing, and demanding ministry.

Thanks to my dedicated staff for their labor of love alongside me, and the people of my church for their prayers, support, and suggestions.

Thanks to Jeff Gerke and Delores Jones for their editing.

Thanks to Gloria Myers from WinePress Publishing.

My sincere thanks to men of God who have supported me and this book.

Contents

Author's Preface

This book grew out of a series called "Family Mess," which I preached in 1997 at my church, The House of the LORD, in Akron, Ohio. As I preached single or multiple messages from this series at other churches, I've been greatly humbled and amazed by the number of people who have experienced the healing touch of God through these teachings. The demand for tapes and requests for sermon notes revealed the need to put this series into book form.

These twelve chapters, each with discussion questions, are ideal for quarterly Sunday school studies or home Bible groups.

I pray that God will use this book to help you acknowledge the fact that family mess happens. I pray that by acknowledging this the Holy Spirit will bring to your remembrance painful events that need to be felt, processed, grieved, forgiven, and released. I pray that this process will bring you face-to-face with the living God, with the realization that He is greater than family mess, and that He works in spite of, through, beneath, above, and beyond family mess to give you an eternal destiny!

Chapter One

The Long-Term Impact of Family Mess
(As the World Turns)

The longer I live, the more I learn. The more I learn, the more I know that there is to learn. The more that I see that there is to learn, the more I realize how little time I have to learn what God wants me to learn and apply.

One of the truths that has greatly impacted me concerns the long-term impact of families upon their members. This impact can be good or bad, but the negative impact is particularly devastating. This is poignantly pointed out in the Bible. Four times the Word of God states:

> You shall not make for yourself an idol, or any likeness of what is in heaven above or on the earth beneath or in the water under the earth. You shall not worship them or serve them; for I, the LORD your God, am a jealous God, *visiting the iniquity of the fathers on the children, on the third and the fourth generations of those who hate Me.* (Exodus 20:4–5, emphasis mine)

Then the LORD passed by in front of him and proclaimed, "The LORD, the LORD God, compassionate and gracious, slow to anger, and abounding in lovingkindness and truth; who keeps lovingkindness for thousands, who forgives iniquity, transgression and sin; yet He will by no means leave the guilty unpunished, *visiting the iniquity of fathers on the children and on the grandchildren to the third and fourth generations.*" (Exodus 34:6–7, emphasis mine)

The LORD is slow to anger and abundant in lovingkindness, forgiving iniquity and transgression; but He will by no means clear the guilty, *visiting the iniquity of the fathers on the children to the third and the fourth generations.*" (Numbers 14:18, emphasis mine)

You shall not make for yourself an idol, or any likeness of what is in heaven above or on the earth beneath or in the water under the earth. You shall not worship them or serve them; for I, the LORD your God, am a jealous God, *visiting the iniquity of the fathers on the children, and on the third and the fourth generations of those who hate Me.*" (Deuteronomy 5:8–9, emphasis mine)

As you can see, the operative phrase is "visiting the iniquity of the fathers on the children to the third and fourth generations." This is the phrase I will concentrate on.

First, we need to determine what God is *not* saying. He is not saying that He punishes the children for the sin of their parents. He clearly says so in Deuteronomy 24:16— "Fathers shall not be put to death for their sons, nor shall sons be put to death for their fathers; everyone shall be put to death for his own sin."

So, what *is* God saying?

Well, let's look at the meaning of the words to see if we can begin to understand what God is saying. First, the Hebrew word for *visiting* is *paqad,* which means to visit, either with friendly or hostile intent. Second, the Hebrew word for *iniquity* is *avon,* which means perversity, moral evil, fault, iniquity, mischief, punishment of iniquity, or sin.[1]

So, God is saying that He is going to visit, or bring about, punishment for the sinfulness of a father to the third and fourth generation of that man's family. The word *punishment* in this context does not mean the inflicting of a penalty upon one for a crime or sin, but the suffering, pain, or loss that serves as retribution. God is not discussing the punishment of a penalty, but the consequences of sin. Let's examine this closely.

God must, because of His nature, deal retribution to every human being. The word *retribution* means "just punishment for evil done or just reward for good done." So retribution can be either positive or negative, depending upon the context. At the end of time, when God wraps everything up, He will give to every person his or her retribution. God must do this because of His immutable, unchanging, stable nature.

God is a holy God. He is a just God. He is a righteous God. Therefore, every sin must receive a just payment of reward, recompense, or retribution. Like the word *retribution,* the meaning of the words *recompense* and *reward,* when they are used in the Bible, must be determined by their usage.

Since we are all sinners and our *self*-righteousness is nothing more than filthy rags, we must be sentenced to hell to pay for our sins. This is tragic indeed, but praise God that the Cross takes care of all sins—past, present, and future with respect to salvation—of those who place their trust in

Jesus Christ. Jesus' death upon the cross takes care of the penalty of sin for those who place their faith in Him.

However, in the four passages of Scripture, quoted above, God is not discussing personal sin, but *familial* sin. God is discussing the impact of sin upon succeeding generations. He is referring to the consequences of sin, both forgiven and unforgiven, upon the children who will come later.

Though the wonderful gift of God's forgiveness takes care of all sin—past, present, and future—with respect to salvation, it does not wipe out the *consequences* of sin in this life. One day God will right every wrong and wipe away every tear from our eyes, but for now the consequences of sin are still with us. Therefore God must, because of His nature, visit the consequences of the father's sin upon the children to the third and fourth generation.

There is another reason why God must visit the consequences of the sins of fathers upon their children: God's nature is expressed in the laws of the earth that He has created.

For instance, Newton's Third Law of Motion says that for every action there is an equal and opposite reaction. In the same way, there are consequences for righteousness and sin, and these consequences must be visited upon future generations. The Scriptures we are considering deal with the consequences for sin. It is not so much God personally visiting the consequences of sin upon succeeding generations as it is the nature of the way that God has created things to operate—which is in keeping with His own nature.

Salvation takes care of the punishment for sin, but it does not take care of the specific impact of sin. Consequences are the normal, logical, natural, systematic results of an action—basically cause and effect. For every cause there is some effect:

- If a fertile man and woman have sex, the effect is often a baby.
- If someone chooses to drink heavily for a long period of time, the effect is often cirrhosis of the liver.
- If a father or mother commits sin, the effect is that some consequences of that sin will show up in their children in some way.

This is a law of heredity. Because of the disobedience of Adam, the stream of Humanity is polluted and we all inherit the sin nature. We are born in the sin that has been passed on to us from our parents, grandparents, etc. But how? Well, I'm no scientist, but I do know that Humanity has come far enough in scientific study to know that genes control inheritance by transmitting one or more traits to one's offspring. The genes of the father are passed on to his offspring. In those genes is the genetic code of the father, which may actually include specific sinful impact. This is also true of the mother's genes, although we are presently discussing the father.

We've all seen someone who has not grown up with his father or ever known him but acts just like him. How can that be? How can a boy act so much like a father he has never known? It's because the father's traits have been genetically passed on to him. This has been proven scientifically.

This brings us to the age-old question: What causes people to sin—their heredity (that which is inborn) or their environment (that which they experience)? We shall see in the chapters to come that the answer is *both*. Children are impacted by the consequences of the father's sin through both heredity and environmental influences. The degree of impact depends upon many variables, but one thing is sure:

the consequences of a father's sin will impact his offspring. Therefore, we are beginning to see what God means when the Bible says He visits the iniquity (i.e. the consequences of sin) of the fathers upon the children to the third and fourth generations.

Perhaps the most striking aspect of this truth is that sin has such far-reaching, long-term effects. Keep in mind these three familial impacts of sin:

1. *Sin always effects present devastation and bondage.* The sins of the father and the mother bring devastation and bondage to both themselves and their children.

2. *Sin always reaches back to the past.* Present sin is somehow connected to past sin through heredity or environmental influence. Sin is never a single act, disconnected from the larger continuum of human sin. Our sinful acts are connected to past generations, all the way back to Adam. This entire sequence of events began in the Garden of Eden.

3. *Sin never stops with one generation.* Sin always reaches forward and touches our future posterity—our children. It always impacts the generations to come.

An excellent Minirth/Meier book entitled *Kids Who Carry Our Pain* accurately states that our children deal with and finish the pain that we didn't work through in our own lives. But I take that one step further: Kids not only carry our pain, *they also carry the consequences of our sin.* Much of that pain results from the consequences of our sin.

This is easy to understand when you consider devastating sins like physical, emotional, sexual, drug, and alcohol abuse. It's also true, but much harder to see and understand, with sins like gluttony, stinginess, or fantasy.

Clearly and undeniably: family sin leads to family mess! When we say something is a mess, we mean that the situation is disorderly, confusing, muddled, troubling, difficult, untidy, dirty, and thus embarrassing. Disorder means a lack of normal order, suggesting an upset of the normal functions or health of something. Consequently, "mess" is strongly related to the concept of dysfunctionality. Family sin leads to family dysfunction: It's a family mess!

Families in a mess have three rules that every member usually follows:

1. *Don't talk.* Never tell anyone about the sin, abuse, or neglect that is going on or has gone on in your family. Keep the family secrets. Generally, the sicker the family, the more secrets that must be kept. I am not discussing the normal privacy of a healthy family, but the sick privacy of abuse.

2. *Don't feel.* Do whatever you must to avoid facing the pain of your situation. Use whatever substance, pattern, person, thing, or idea you need to keep the pain away. Don't face the pain because it will undo you. You just want to go on. But you can't gloss over family mess! It has to be dealt with. When Nehemiah came to Jerusalem, not only were the walls broken down and the gates burned with fire, but there was also debris in the street. That debris had to be dealt with. You can't build a city on debris—you need to clean up first. Likewise, family mess needs to be dealt with.

3. *Don't trust.* You have been so devastated that you can't afford to trust anyone, no matter how trustworthy a person might be or how he might prove himself. This includes God! The thinking is, "If people are untrustworthy, God must be, too."

Family Mess

Family mess is a part of life. Family mess happens, even "As the World Turns!" It's not something you can avoid, but it is something that you can heal from.

The Bible is a real book that gives the real story of real people and their real interaction with the real God! Therefore, the Bible is full of family mess. God does not hide the truth! He deals with reality. There can be no healing or freedom from family mess until we face the reality of what has happened.

Take slavery, for instance. It's interesting to me that few people seem to understand the ongoing impact of slavery upon the African-American community, people, and family. Going back three or four generations in our history, we come face-to-face with the ravages of the American brand of slavery, which was one of the most dehumanizing forms known to humanity.

The family mess caused by slavery still impacts us today. We still don't talk very freely; we still have difficulty feeling our real feelings; and we still have trouble trusting one another—not to mention other ethnic groups.

But praise God, because He wants to deliver us from family mess. He has a lot of experience in delivering people from the family mess of slavery: He delivered His own people, the Israelites, who had been in bondage in Egypt for 400 years!

God took the children of Israel out of Egypt in one night, but it took Him forty years to wean the impacts of Egyptian slavery out of the children of Israel. Even after the adults of that generation had died, the people were still suffering the long-term impacts of their previous slavery. I don't bring this up to make excuses for African-American people. I bring this up so that we may understand the reality of the damage that has occurred and realistically seek God for deliverance and healing.

In His deliverance, God used both the *crisis* and the *process* of deliverance.

- *Deliverance from Egypt was a crisis.* It happened miraculously, in one night, at once—and once and for all. God closed the Red Sea behind them so they couldn't go back.
- *Deliverance from the effects of slavery was a process.* It took at least forty years in the wilderness, and probably more time in the Promised Land.

God delivered African-Americans from the Egypt of slavery with the Emancipation Proclamation, though the Emancipation Proclamation has never been fully realized. Deliverance is a process. Therefore, we are still struggling with the effects of slavery.

God took us out of the slavery of sin in the *crisis* of salvation. Jesus said that "if the Son makes you free, you will be free indeed" (John 8:36), but we are still struggling with the effects of sin. God is still taking slavery out of us in the *process* of progressive sanctification.

"As the World Turns" there is sin, family mess, and generational bondage. But there is a God who wants to bring hope, deliverance, and restoration!

Family mess can also be a divine messenger with a divine message!

- *God uses the suffering of our ethnicity to deliver a divine message of hope, deliverance, and restoration to the world.* When the world looks at African-American people and sees the hope, deliverance, and restoration that God has worked in us after the suffering of slavery, it is a testimony to the power of Almighty God.

- *God uses the suffering of our ethnicity to deliver a divine message of compassion, deep feeling, devotion, and piety to this world.* God wants the world to look on Black people, see our suffering, and understand what compassion is all about.

- *God uses the suffering of our ethnicity to create "trans-ethnic" communities to model love and reconciliation.* He wants to show the world what a true microcosm of heaven would look like; red, yellow, black and white, worshiping God here on earth, right now—through the power of the Holy Spirit ("Transethnic" coined by Jack Hayford).

Let me summarize this chapter with five important truths:

1. *Family mess is the tip-off that there is something seriously wrong with your family.* Don't ignore it or say, "Well, you know, that's just the way we are." Pay attention to it.

2. *Family mess is the tip-off that there is something beyond natural circumstances impacting your family: generational bondage.* When you remember that your great-grandfather was an alcoholic, and that your grandfather was an alcoholic, and that your father was an alcoholic, you need to pay attention to that pattern.

3. *Family mess is the tip-off that you need someone or something greater than yourself, if you are going to be healed.* Counseling is necessary, but only Jesus Christ can truly straighten out family mess.

4. *Family mess can alert you to areas of struggle or sin that you should be aware of.* This is similar to point number two. If you're a woman and your great-grandmother,

grandmother, and mother always had three or four men hanging around, guess what sin you should watch out for in your own life?

5. *Family mess can alert you to areas of struggle or sin where God wants to work.* He wants to move right in at the deepest, most difficult part of your life to bring healing and transformation.

In the next chapter, we will follow the "mess" in the family of God's chosen people, beginning with the patriarch Abraham. We will see the impact of family mess as well as how God works to establish His chosen people in spite of it.

Discussion Questions

1. Why must God visit the consequences of the fathers' sins upon their children? Please answer this question in your own words.

2. Are you aware of any family mess in your family? Can you share an experience that has negatively impacted your formation as a person?

3. How are you keeping or breaking the three big rules of family dysfunctionality?

4. Can you get in touch with anything that God might be trying to work out through the suffering of your particular family mess?

5. Can you think of any biblical or daily situation where God has given someone a destiny in spite of family mess?

---

1. *Strong's Greek and Hebrew Dictionary* (Database c. 1990-93 NavPress Software).

Chapter Two

The Process of Separation from Family Mess
(The Guiding Light)

In the first chapter, we saw that family sin leads to family mess. God must visit the consequences of the sins of the fathers upon the children. However, while this is certainly true, this does not necessarily cause family mess. So, what does cause family mess?

Let's touch on two probable causes:

1. Human depravity
2. Satan and his evil horde

Let's talk first about human depravity. Having the consequences of hereditary and environmental sin passed on to anyone is very serious, but human depravity makes it family mess. Heredity and environmental forces are not the sole, or even the primary, determining factors in how a person will turn out.

We have bought into this idea that we're all messed up because of either our genes or our homes. But I say there's something else behind our family mess.

The determining factor is still human will and choice. God holds us accountable for our choices even though we face some powerful influences. Don't worry, He knows that we are but dust! But, it is human depravity impacting our human will and choices that makes family mess.

Because of the fall—the sin of Adam who is the father of Humanity—the entire human race is depraved (utterly sinful). Paul, speaking for God, put it this way:

> As it is written, "There is none righteous, not even one; there is none who understands, there is none who seeks for God; all have turned aside, together they have become useless; there is none who does good, there is not even one." (Romans 3:10–12)

It's true that we all receive the consequences of our forefathers' sins. But it's our own depravity or utter wickedness that causes our individual *expression* of family mess. Our choices will be in keeping with the unique nature of our own personal depravity. Without Jesus Christ and the ongoing sanctifying ministry of the Holy Spirit, our choices cannot help but produce family mess.

This does not mean that there is nothing noble in human beings, because the image of God is still inside of us. But we are fallen image-bearers!

There is also another very powerful reason for family mess: the devil. We have an enemy and his name is Satan. Because he is God's enemy; he is our enemy. He is hell bent on taking the sin and the opportunities we give him and turning them into family mess in our lives. God allows this for His own sovereign purposes and His own ultimate, divine glory, until He brings everything to consummation at the end of the age.

I hope that, "visiting the iniquity of the fathers upon the children to the third and fourth generation" is becoming clearer to you. I want you to realize the force behind it, and its tremendous impact.

Now we'll take a look at how this phrase worked its way out in the family of Abraham. The Bible gives us the important details of the life of Abraham. Malcolm Smith said this in his book, *Spiritual Burnout:*

> The Scripture is not a book of systematic theology that tabulates what we are to believe. It is a book of biographies that show how very ordinary people through the ages have learned to walk in God's strength to overcome their problems. He shows how they discovered the reality of God in the black holes of their personal failures.[1]

Abraham was the friend of God. He was chosen by God to be a great example of faith, the father of many nations, the father of the Israelites, and the father of the genealogical line of the Messiah, Jesus Christ.

> Now these are the records of the generations of Terah. Terah became the father of Abram, Nahor and Haran; and Haran became the father of Lot. Haran died in the presence of his father Terah in the land of his birth, in Ur of the Chaldeans. Abram and Nahor took wives for themselves. The name of Abram's wife was Sarai; and the name of Nahor's wife was Milcah, the daughter of Haran, the father of Milcah and Iscah. Sarai was barren; she had no child. Terah took Abram his son, and Lot the son of Haran, his grandson, and Sarai his daughter-in-law, his son Abram's wife; and they went out together from Ur of the Chaldeans in order to enter the land of Canaan; and they went as far as Haran, and settled there.

The days of Terah were two hundred and five years; and Terah died in Haran.

Now the Lord said to Abram, "Go forth from your country, And from your relatives And from your father's house, To the land which I will show you; And I will make you a great nation, And I will bless you, And make your name great; And so you shall be a blessing; And I will bless those who bless you, And the one who curses you I will curse. And in you all the families of the earth will be blessed."

So Abram went forth as the Lord had spoken to him; and Lot went with him. Now Abram was seventy-five years old when he departed from Haran. Abram took Sarai his wife and Lot his nephew, and all their possessions which they had accumulated, and the persons which they had acquired in Haran, and they set out for the land of Canaan; thus they came to the land of Canaan. (Genesis 11:27–12:5)

Here we have the background of Abraham. (His name was actually Abram at this point, since this was before God changed his name to Abraham. But for convenience and familiarity, let's call him Abraham.) Here we see the Lord God's call upon his life, and here the family sin begins.

Ur of the Chaldeans was in ancient Babylonia, where the worship of idols and false gods was quite prominent. We know from Joshua 24:2 that Terah, Abraham's father, served other gods. Remember, family sin leads to family mess! But God stepped into the midst of this family sin, this idolatry, and called Abraham. God gave Abraham something that no one in his family had apparently experienced before: "A Guiding Light." The Guiding Light of God was His Word and His promises.

Jehovah God actually gave Abraham three promises and reminded him of a fourth:

1. great reward
2. a son to be his heir
3. his descendants being as numerous as the stars
4. a reminder of an earlier promise of possessing the land as an inheritance.

God was actually calling Abraham to rise above family sin and family mess.

Praise God that when we were bound in the family mess of our family tree, He provided The Guiding Light of the Gospel of Jesus Christ. If you have accepted Jesus Christ as your personal Savior, you have accepted the call of God to rise above family mess. If you have not accepted Jesus Christ as your personal Savior, you still can!

God does not want us to be bound by family mess. He does not want us bound by the sins of our fathers. We are bound by the sins of our fathers because of Adam's sin, our own depravity, and Satan's lies. But God wants to deliver us from family mess, and in so doing bring glory to His holy name. God wants us to rise above family mess.

God wanted Abraham to rise above family sin and family mess, too, but to do so Abraham would have to obey God in three areas:

1. He would have to leave his country.
2. He would have to leave his relatives.
3. He would have to leave his father's house.

If we are going to rise above our own family mess and become the men and women that God wants us to become, we will have to first obey God. There are no exceptions. There are no exemptions or shortcuts. Not only do we have to obey God if we are going to rise above family mess, but we must obey God in the same three areas. Let's look at them more closely.

If Abraham was going to rise above family mess and obey God, he had to leave his country. This meant leaving a very familiar place for one that was totally unfamiliar. God would not reveal the place to Abraham, until after he left home. If Abraham was going to pull this off, he had to trust God.

We've come to look at faith as intellectual assent to ideas or concepts, but it's much more than that. Faith, in the Bible, is trust in God. Abraham's faith required a trust in God that allowed him to abandon himself to and rest in God's promises. He could only do that if he trusted the character of Jehovah God.

If we are going to rise above family mess and obey God, we must trust God. Faith is our abandonment to and rest in God's promises. God will not fully reveal His destiny for us, until we leave home.

Now maybe you're saying, "I've already left home." Not so fast! You haven't left home if every time your mother says something upsetting to you, it bothers you the rest of the week. You haven't left home if you are still trying to gain your father's approval. Even if your parents are dead you may still be "at home." If they are still controlling your decisions from beyond the grave, you have not left home. Nevertheless, we have God's promises, in spite of family mess.

- *God promised to love us with an everlasting love* (Jeremiah 31:3; John 15:9). Sometimes we are battered by this world and begin to think that God has removed His love from us, but faith is abandonment to and rest in His promise.

- *God promised that He would never let us be tempted beyond what we are able to bear* (1 Corinthians 10:13). We can always look back at the end of our trials and say that He didn't overburden us, but in the middle it's not always so clear. So, again, faith is abandonment to and rest in that promise.

- *God promised to conform us to the image of His dear Son* (Romans 8:29). There are times in the Christian life when the sun seems to be blotted out. We know it's back there, but we can't see it and can't feel its warmth. So, we learn again that faith is abandonment to and rest in God's promise.

- *God promised that He would never leave us or forsake us* (Hebrews 13:5). There are times when He seems to be hiding, but we choose to believe that He is there still. This is the testing of our faith, and faith is abandonment to and rest in that promise.

- *God promised to come back to get us one day (1 Thessalonians 4:16–17).* We look around and can't find any hint that He's about to return, but He said He was, so that settles it. We come to know that faith is abandonment to and rest in God's promises.

If Abraham was to rise above family mess and become the man that God wanted him to become by obeying and trusting God, he had to leave home.

Abraham was probably living in his father's tents. This was not unusual for the nomadic people of those times, but God wanted to do something new with Abraham. He wanted Abraham to leave his father's house and all his relatives. He knew that Abraham would never escape the influence of family mess as long as he lived in such close proximity to it. God had a vision for Abraham's life, but Abraham would have to accept that vision by obeying and trusting Him.

God wants to do something miraculous in the lives of every one of His children. He has a destiny for each one of us, but in order to receive the miracle and destiny of God, we must leave home.

- We must get finished with our "mother issues."

- We must tear down our fathers' altars.

- We must leave home volitionally, physically, intellectually, emotionally, and spiritually.

- We must leave home and all of its issues and press on towards the mark of the prize of the high calling of God in Christ Jesus.

God has a vision for our lives. To release that vision, we must accept God's vision for us no matter how we look to ourselves or to someone else.

We now have a glimpse of the family sin that was impacting Abraham and the call of God upon his life. In the passage of Scripture that we are considering, we see that the family mess got started when Abraham partially obeyed God.

Steven's sermon in Acts 7 seems to indicate that Abraham had a hard time leaving his country and his father's home. It appears that he didn't actually leave until after his father died. It's possible that Abraham didn't obey God's Word immediately.

Whether Abraham left home before or after his father's death, his disobedience in the situation with Lot is clear. We don't know how or why it happened, but his nephew, Lot, went with him. The Bible gives two scenarios:

It says that Lot went with him.

It also says that Abraham took Lot with him.

The Hebrew word for *took* can also mean *accept*, so it's hard to say. It seems that Lot wanted to go with Abraham, and Abraham didn't have the heart to tell him, "You can't go with me, because that is God's Word." In the vernacular of today's pop psychology, Abraham was codependent or dysfunctional. He couldn't say *no* to Lot. He couldn't set the proper boundaries where Lot was concerned.

But the problem was much larger than that. Abraham partially disobeyed God. Abraham, one of the major New Testament examples of faith, demonstrated from the beginning that he had trouble trusting God. This is important in our understanding of how Abraham came to be a great example of faith. His faith did not flow from his natural self, but from the transforming power of the Holy Spirit.

Why did Abraham have trouble trusting God? I think the answer lies in his family sin. Abraham had come from a home and a country where false gods were worshiped. He was learning to have a relationship with the true and living God. Trusting God would be a problem for Abraham over the course of his life, but God would eventually transform him into a shining example of faith. God had a vision and plan for Abraham, and not even family sin could thwart that plan—if Abraham would trust and obey.

God wanted to use Abraham, but He would first have to separate Abraham from his relatives. When Abraham allowed Lot to go with him, he allowed family mess to travel along with him.

Family mess gets started in our lives when we disobey God because of another family member.

- We don't know how to set boundaries.
- We don't know how to say *no* to someone we love.
- We don't know how to obey God because of a difficult situation with a relative.

I wouldn't have a church today if I hadn't learned how to say *no* at certain points to people who were close to me. Not "No, I don't care"; not "No, I don't want to be bothered with you"; but "No, this is not the will of God. I must follow God's will. I cannot do what you want me to do. I don't care how good that looks, how it looks like it will straighten out the problem, or how it seems that it'll all work out. If I don't do what God tells me to do, we're going to have a serious problem. So, I must say *no.*"

If you're a married man, have you ever had to say *no* to your wife? Have you ever had God tell you one thing and your wife tell you something else? Abraham had a hard time with that. His wife told him one thing, and he felt he had to do what she said. Adam had a hard time with that, too. I think most men have a hard time with that.

If you're a married woman, have you ever had to say *no* when your husband's tells you, "I want you to do this" but God's saying, "I want you to do something else"? There are situations in life when we've got to say *no!* But it's very difficult, isn't it?

When I was growing up, I attended Shelton Temple Church of God in Christ, in Akron, Ohio, pastored by Bishop Olethus E. Shelton. Bishop Shelton once gave me some words of advice that I shall never forget. After some discussion about a difficult decision, he said to me, "Brother Joey, what do you want to be, a woodchopper or a chip-gatherer?" As a teenager, I didn't fully understand what he was asking. Nevertheless, I knew enough to know that I wanted to be a woodchopper. So I said, "A woodchopper, I guess." He said, "Then chop the wood and let the chips fall where they may!"

You can't be a woodchopper and a chip-gatherer at the same time. You either have to chop the wood and forget about the chips or you can try to keep the chips from flying and never chop the wood.

There are times in family relationships when we need to chop the wood of God and let the chips fall where they may. But most of us often try to keep the chips from flying and hitting our relatives. We try to obey God and please relatives at the same time. That is often impossible.

I've decided I want to be a woodchopper for Jesus Christ. I'm going to chop the wood by faith. I'm going to obey God by faith. I'm going to chop God's wood and let the chips of circumstances, misunderstanding, and criticism fall where they may. God is in control and He will take care of the location of the chips.

When we try to keep chips from hitting our relatives, we still often end up in trouble with them—and the wood of God unchopped.

There comes a time when God calls us to grow up emotionally and spiritually, and God calls us to go out with Him and leave our relatives behind. We may even have to let our children go, because they will bring along their family mess. It is through an intimate relationship with the LORD that He wants to deliver us from family mess. When we let our relatives travel with us, against the direct commandments of God, we allow family mess to travel with us and we can never get free.

God's has a wonderful purpose, plan, and vision for your life, but it may mean separation from your relatives and their family mess. What do you want to be—a woodchopper or a chip-gatherer?

Discussion Questions

1. How is your own unique form of human depravity expressing itself in your family mess?

2. Compare God's vision for your life with your vision for yourself.

3. Can you identify any relative or friend that God may be trying to separate you from emotionally?

4. How are you doing with the obedience and trust necessary to chop the wood?

5. What chips might you be trying to gather up with reference to a relative?

1. Malcolm Smith, *Spiritual Burnout* (Tulsa, Oklahoma: Pillar Books and Publishing Company, 1995), 86.

Chapter Three

The Separation of Abraham and Lot
(As the World Turns 2)

Family mess happens, even as the world turns. Previously, we saw the beginning of family mess in Abraham's family, when he allowed Lot to travel with him—against the expressed Word of God, the Guiding Light. Now let's see how the mess unfolds:

> So Abram went up from Egypt to the Negev, he and his wife and all that belonged to him, and Lot went with him. Now Abram was very rich in livestock, in silver and in gold.

> He went on his journeys from the Negev as far as Bethel, to the place where his tent had been at the beginning, between Bethel and Ai, to the place of the altar which he had made there formerly; and there Abram called on the name of the LORD.

> Now Lot, who went with Abram, also had flocks and herds and tents. And the land could not sustain them while dwelling together, for their possessions were so

great that they were not able to remain together. And there was strife between the herdsmen of Abram's livestock and the herdsmen of Lot's livestock. Now the Canaanite and the Perizzite were dwelling then in the land.

So Abram said to Lot, "Please let there be no strife between you and me, nor between my herdsmen and your herdsmen, for we are brothers. Is not the whole land before you? Please separate from me; if to the left, then I will go to the right; or if to the right, then I will go to the left."

Lot lifted up his eyes and saw all the valley of the Jordan, that it was well watered everywhere—this was before the LORD destroyed Sodom and Gomorrah-like the garden of the LORD, like the land of Egypt as you go to Zoar. So Lot chose for himself all the valley of the Jordan, and Lot journeyed eastward. Thus they separated from each other. Abram settled in the land of Canaan, while Lot settled in the cities of the valley, and moved his tents as far as Sodom. Now the men of Sodom were wicked exceedingly and sinners against the LORD.

The LORD said to Abram, after Lot had separated from him, "Now lift up your eyes and look from the place where you are, northward and southward and eastward and westward; for all the land which you see, I will give it to you and to your descendants forever. I will make your descendants as the dust of the earth, so that if anyone can number the dust of the earth, then your descendants can also be numbered. Arise, walk about the land through its length and breadth; for I will give it to you." Then Abram moved his tent and came and dwelt by the oaks of Mamre, which are in Hebron, and there he built an altar to the LORD. (Genesis 13:1–18)

In the phrase, "and Lot went with him," we learn that Abraham only partially obeyed God. We learn that Abraham was codependent or dysfunctional. Codependency is when you can only live your life through somebody else's. Some people don't like psychological terms, so let me put it biblically: Abraham sinned. He couldn't say *no* to Lot. He couldn't set the proper boundaries where Lot was concerned.

Isn't that where a great deal of our problems start: when we fail to obey God with respect to separation from a family member? God has a special mission for every one of His children, and He often separates us unto Himself to prepare us for it.

This principle of *separation for preparation* is seen in many places in the Bible. Let's just note three:

- *God prepared Moses on the backside of the desert* (Exodus 3:1–12). Separated from all of humanity, God manifested Himself to Moses and commissioned him to lead the Children of Israel out of Egypt.
- *God prepared Jesus in the wilderness* (Matthew 4:1–11). After forty days of temptation in the wilderness, Jesus was ready to begin His public ministry.
- *God separated John to the Isle of Patmos* (Revelation 1:9–11). There on Patmos, God gave John the Revelation of the end times.

Before God can use us, sometimes He has to separate us unto Himself to prepare us for service. This can be a problem for people who can't handle being alone. They turn on the TV or the radio or go out into public to escape being alone. But how can God deal with us, if He can never get us alone to Himself?

Remember when you were dating? How you wanted to get your date all alone, right? You didn't want brothers, sisters, mother, father or anybody to come along with you, you wanted that special person all to yourself. Likewise, God wants you all to Himself, too.

But sometimes, when God wants to separate us unto Himself, we try to take family members with us—family members whom God has asked us to emotionally separate from. Consider Abraham and Lot.

Though I've touched on the reason for the separation of Lot from Abraham, there's still the question of why God wouldn't allow Lot to remain with Abraham. There are probably other reasons, but I think primarily Lot represented a link to Abraham's family, which we know worshiped idols.

The same can be true of us. God may want to separate us emotionally from family members who represent a link to our codependent, dysfunctional, idolatrous family systems, and family of origin issues.

While that is certainly a good reason for such a separation, the problem is much deeper than that. God wanted Abraham, a future example of faith and trust in God, to place his full trust in Him. Yet Abraham had trouble trusting Jehovah God. God knew that Abraham's codependency and lack of trust in Him would lead to more family mess. God needed to separate Lot from Abraham so that He could mold Abraham into the faithful, obedient servant who would one day receive a fantastic destiny.

God knows that our codependency and inability to trust Him will lead to more family mess. It will block His plans to make us what He wants us to be and to give us a fantastic destiny. So, He sometimes has to separate us from a family member that has a toxic effect upon us.

Over and over in the Bible we come face-to-face with two major prerequisites to a vibrant, Spirit-filled, successful life: faith and obedience. "Trust and obey!" Salvation is through trust, and we walk by faith or trust. Obedience is one of the greatest biblical commands, because it illustrates our love of Jehovah God.

In Genesis 13 we see the progress of Abraham's journey. In the previous chapter, the LORD had told him:

> Go forth from your country, and from your relatives and from your father's house, to the land which I will show you; and I will make you a great nation, and I will bless you, and make your name great; and so you shall be a blessing; and I will bless those who bless you, and the one who curses you I will curse. And in you all the families of the earth will be blessed. (Genesis 12:1–3)

Abraham was exchanging:

- his country for the Promised Land;
- his natural relatives for God-given relatives; and
- his father's house for the house of his heavenly Father.

But, this was all dependent upon Abraham's trust in and obedience to Jehovah God. Here are three applications of this truth:

1. *God wants us to exchange our father's country for the promised land of abundant Christian living.* Our father's country maybe a land of bondage to the idolatry of alcoholism, but in the Promised Land we are free to worship the true and living God. God wants us to exchange bondage

for freedom, a fleshly walk for a Spirit-filled walk, and punishment for reward.

2. *God wants us to exchange our relatives for the family of God.* He wants us to give up our Adamic family for the body of Jesus Christ. We don't have to treat them badly or refuse to talk to people in our natural, human families, but they cannot get between us and the wood-chopping that God has assigned to our hands.

3. *God wants us to exchange faith in our natural fathers and ancestry for faith in Him as our heavenly Father and our heavenly ancestry.* Paul's words capture this point beautifully: "For we are the true circumcision, who worship in the Spirit of God and glory in Christ Jesus and *put no confidence in the flesh*" (Philippians 3:3, emphasis mine). Our confidence is in Jesus Christ, not the flesh—neither ours nor our family members'.

As Abraham continued his sojourn, he came upon the place where he had previously built an altar. There he began to call upon the name of the LORD. Abraham had a custom of building an altar every time He encountered God or something of great spiritual significance occurred. These altars were meant as memorials and for worship. Every time Abraham came across one of his altars, he was reminded of what God had done for him and he was inspired to worship God anew.

We too should build worship markers to remember and celebrate anew our encounters with and blessings of Jehovah God. When we come across the markers and are reminded of what God did, we should call upon His name and worship Him afresh.

Now we come to the culmination of the family mess that Abraham brought on by allowing Lot to travel with him. As Abraham journeyed toward the Promised Land, Abraham's herdsmen and Lot's herdsmen began quarreling. As the world turns, family mess happens! Abraham and Lot were both rich. They each had a lot of livestock, and the land could not support both herds. Now, had Abraham trusted and obeyed God, he would not have let Lot travel with him and would have avoided this whole family mess.

Oh, what problems Abraham brought upon himself and his family when he chose to distrust and disobey God! This was not the blatant sin of commission, but the sin of omission. It wasn't so much what Abraham did that got them all in trouble, but what he didn't do. Abraham disobeyed God by failing to do what He wanted him to do.

We can be like that, too. Sometimes we sit when we should be doing something. In being passive, we end up letting the will of God go undone. That's a sin of omission. Oh, what family mess we bring upon ourselves when we choose to distrust and disobey God! We bring great pain and misery into our lives through negligence and sins of omission, particularly when we fail to set boundaries with our family members.

Now Abraham has to solve this mess with Lot. He told Lot about his values and pleaded that they should not be fighting, because they were relatives. Then Abraham, trying to avoid family mess, offered Lot a solution. He said, in effect, "Go wherever you want to go. Take the best land, if you want, and I will take whatever's left" (Genesis 13:8–9). Abraham was willing to take a loss so that there might be peace between him and his nephew.

Is this a good or a bad thing? Abraham's offer may be a manifestation of his biblical values and his passivity. I will explore Abraham's passivity in a later chapter, so let's consider the biblical values that he revealed in this situation.

The biblical values that I feel Abraham portrayed are love, peace, and personal sacrifice—principles that we should strive to emulate and practice in our lives. We should love others, particularly family members, and consider them better than ourselves. We should be willing to suffer loss for the sake of peace.

As I pointed out in chapter one, although family mess can be very painful and destructive, it can alert us to areas of struggle or sin where God wants to work. Abraham struggled in trusting Jehovah God. This family mess with Lot gave Abraham an opportunity to learn to trust in God and manifest that trust through obedience and love.

Likewise, God often uses family mess as an opportunity for us to live out and demonstrate our Christianity. So when we see family mess starting to happen, we should start looking for a personal area of struggle to see how God wants to work on us, in us, and through us.

When you see family mess in your family—and as the world turns, it will happen—start looking for a way that you can let the light of Jesus Christ shine through you. When you see at the family reunion that Aunt Mary isn't talking to Cousin Ethel, consider it an opportunity for ministry. It's an opportunity for the lost members of your family to see that there is something different about you, and the difference is Jesus.

At the next funeral, if they start to fight over daddy's stuff, it's time to show the difference between you and them. During the wedding rehearsal, if the groom can't be found, it's a time for you to intercede in family mess and show the difference between you and them. So, the next time you see family mess, instead of running, ask yourself, "How can God use me in this? How can I be what God wants me to be in this? What is God saying to me?"

The Separation of Abraham and Lot

This episode in Abraham's life gives us a much better perspective on why he and Lot needed to be separated: They didn't have the same values and they were not looking for the same things. Abraham's values were more other-oriented. Lot's values were more self-oriented. Abraham was looking for a city whose architect and builder is God. Lot was looking for something far different.

Lot lifted up his eyes and saw the valley of Jordan. It was well watered like the Garden of Eden, but it was in the direction of Sodom and Gomorrah. It was farther eastward and in the direction where the rest of the world was traveling. Lot selfishly chose the direction of the world.

When Adam and Eve were expelled from the Garden of Eden, they were expelled to the east:

> So He drove the man out; and at the east of the garden of Eden He stationed the cherubim and the flaming sword which turned every direction to guard the way to the tree of life. (Genesis 3:24)

Not only were Adam and Eve expelled to the east of Eden, but it also seems that their offspring and all of Humanity were moving in the same direction.

- "Then Cain went out from the presence of the LORD, and settled in the land of Nod, east of Eden" (Genesis 4:16).

- "It came about as they journeyed east, that they found a plain in the land of Shinar and settled there" (Genesis 11:2).

- "Then he proceeded from there to the mountain on the east of Bethel, and pitched his tent, with Bethel on the west and Ai on the east; and there he built an altar to the LORD and called upon the name of the LORD" (Genesis 12:8).

- "So Lot chose for himself all the valley of the Jordan, and Lot journeyed eastward. Thus they separated from each other" (Genesis 13:11).

It seems that the whole world was traveling east, which represents the way of the world. All that is in the world is the lust of the flesh, the lust of the eyes, and the boastful pride of life (1 John 2:16). All of these factors were probably operating when Lot chose the well-watered land towards the valley of Jordan. While Abraham was looking for a city whose Builder and Maker is God, Lot was looking for the world.

We see that while Lot goes farther east, Abraham goes west. *Abraham appears to choose to go in the opposite direction from the rest of the world.* He turns his back on the secular, conventional direction and goes in the direction of the LORD.

If we are to be used by God, there are times when we must choose to go in the opposite direction from everyone we know. I've faced this situation many times and will face it many times more, if the LORD delays His coming.

God used family mess to separate Lot from Abraham so that Abraham would go in the direction God wanted. As painful, frustrating, and devastating as family mess can be, God often uses it to separate us from dysfunctional relatives to send us in the direction He wants us to go!

Ask yourself: are there family members that God wants to separate you from? Are there relationships that God wants to separate you from? Not necessarily because of sin, but because God wants to do something great with you and through you—something that He cannot do while you are still mixed up with worldly relatives.

If you won't obey God and voluntarily separate from those relatives, God may use family mess to do the job. There is a price to pay for being used by God. It may cost you some separation, isolation, and pain.

After God separates Lot from Abraham, He begins to speak to Abraham, revealing the land that He had promised to him. God tells Abraham to look northward, southward, eastward, and westward. He says, "All the land which you see, I will give it to you and to your descendants forever" (Genesis 13:15). He told him to walk through the land, because He was going to give it to him.

After Lot is separated from Abraham, God kicks His program into high gear. What can we learn from this?

- God could not or would not talk to Abraham until Abraham trusted Him.

- God could not or would not talk to Abraham until Abraham obeyed Him.

- God could not or would not talk to Abraham until He separated him from Lot unto Himself.

- God could not or would not reaffirm His promises to Abraham until he was separated unto Himself.

How does this apply to you?

- Sometimes God cannot or will not speak to you because you have not trusted Him.

- Sometimes God cannot or will not speak to you because you have not obeyed Him.

- Sometimes God cannot or will not speak to you because you have not separated yourself from dysfunctional family members.

After God has separated you unto Himself from worldly relatives, He can give you the promises that He wants you to consider. This is great news: God will work through and beyond family mess to give you His blessed promises. Hallelujah!

There is only one more thing that we need to know: How do we receive the promises of God? The Bible tells us that Abraham traveled a little bit farther, and when he set up his tent he built another altar to the LORD. Every time God did something significant for Abraham, he built an altar and worshiped the LORD. Abraham accepted God's promises through worship.

The only way to accept God's promises is through worship. Once God has used family mess to separate us to Himself and He has reaffirmed His promises to us, the only proper response is worship!

Discussion Questions

1. How has the principle of *separation for preparation* come into play in your life?

2. What does your trust and obedience of Jehovah God look like at this point in your journey?

3. How are you responding to relatives that God may be separating you from?

4. Which way are you traveling in your life: the way of the world or the way of the LORD? How do you know?

5. How is your altar building coming? Recall some previous worship markers that you have set up, and worship God afresh!

Chapter Four

How to Serve Separated Family Members
(The Guiding Light Continued)

We are beginning to see that family mess has a long-term impact upon family members. In this chapter, we will further explore that long-term impact.

We've seen that Lot's choice of the well watered valley of Jordan in the vicinity of Sodom and Gomorrah was self-ish and based on following the direction of the world. Now we'll see that Lot's choice affected his immediate family through generational bondage. We'll also discover more reasons why God separated Lot from Abraham, and see how God continued to work in Lot's life, beyond the family mess.

The background information to this story is very long, so I did not print the entire Scripture text here. I have chosen to summarize the story in my own words. Never-theless, you may want to read the eighteenth and nine-teenth chapters of Genesis before you move into the rest of this chapter.

In Genesis 18, the LORD appeared to Abraham while he was sitting at the door of his tent during the heat of the day. As he lifted up his eyes, he saw three men approaching. We now know that one of the men was God. This was a pre-Bethlehem appearance of our LORD and Savior, Jesus Christ. We can also speculate that the other two men were angels.

Abraham arose to extend the customary Near Eastern hospitality: he prepared a meal for them. As they ate, they asked, "Where is your wife, Sarah?" Then one of them prophesied, "At this time next year, your wife shall have a son." Sarah overheard this. Since she and Abraham were old and she was past the childbearing age, she laughed to herself.

The LORD heard her and asked Sarah, "Why did you laugh? Is anything too difficult for the LORD?" Sarah denied that she had laughed because she was afraid. The LORD then reaffirmed His prophecy concerning a son for Abraham and Sarah at the same time next year.

Now the men rose and started walking in the direction of Sodom, and Abraham walked with them to see them off. We come now to one of those enigmatic passages of Scripture. The LORD said, "Shall I hide what I am about to do from Abraham, since I have a completely different and great destiny for him?"

We don't know who the LORD is talking to, since that is not stated, but He seems to be talking to the other two angels or to Himself. Herein lies the enigma: Why would God ask Himself such a question? God knows all things, right? God already knows everything that He's going to do, right? This is simply an anthropomorphism (attributing human characteristics to God), right? Well, that is a subject for another book.

Whoever God was talking to, it appeared He was considering hiding His intentions from Abraham because Sodom was where Lot lived. Perhaps God didn't want Abraham to be hurt or sidetracked. But, it seems that the

LORD decided to share with Abraham what He was about to do. He said:

> The outcry of Sodom and Gomorrah is indeed great, and their sin is exceedingly grave. I will go down now, and see if they have done entirely according to its outcry, which has come to Me; and if not, I will know. (Genesis 18:20–21)

It seems that God wanted to thoroughly examine the extent of their sin. Once again this does not fit with our concept of God. But that simply means that our concept of God is obviously not completely right.

So, the LORD stood in His place, while the two men went towards Sodom. Now Abraham, understanding what was taking place, approached the LORD and began to bargain for the lives of the people of Sodom, including Lot and his family.

There's a wonderful lesson here. Even though God had separated Lot from Abraham and God had a tremendous destiny for Abraham, Abraham was still concerned about Lot—and rightfully so. His concern was appropriately demonstrated by praying for his nephew, rather than disobeying God by allowing Lot to live with him.

In the last chapter, we saw how God often separates us from sinful, dysfunctional relatives so that He might guide us to our destiny. Here we see how we should respond to separated relatives. We shouldn't dislike them, think we are better than they are or forget about them, because but for the grace of God we could be looking at ourselves. We should intercede with God on their behalf. We should pray for them while they're down in Sodom and Gomorrah.

Now, I have a question for you: Do you have any relatives in Sodom and Gomorrah? Where is Sodom and

Gomorrah? It's on the streets. It's down as deep, as low, and about as far away from God as you can get. It's the last stop before hell. The prodigal son took this same trip. Do you have any relatives there?

Grandfather, grandmother, father, mother, brother, sister, aunt, or uncle: Keep praying for your relatives until God delivers them from Sodom. You may have a relative who is a long way from the tents and altars of Abraham—don't stop praying for him until you see him making his way out of Sodom and Gomorrah.

Let's see what we can learn from Abraham's prayer. As Abraham prayed to God, he began to play on God's justice by asking: "Will You indeed sweep away the righteous with the wicked?" (Genesis 18:23b). In other words, "You're too just to sweep away the righteous with the wicked! You're too just to exact the penalty for sinning upon innocent people."

Then Abraham began to bargain for the lives of the people of Sodom, and his nephew Lot. He asked God,

> Suppose there are fifty righteous within the city; will You indeed sweep it away and not spare the place for the sake of the fifty righteous who are in it? Far be it from You to do such a thing, to slay the righteous with the wicked, so that the righteous and the wicked are treated alike. Far be it from You! Shall not the Judge of all the earth deal justly?
>
> So the Lord said, "If I find in Sodom fifty righteous within the city, then I will spare the whole place on their account." (Genesis 18:24–26)

It seems, at this point, that Abraham realized he was on shaky ground in two areas:

1. *He, being nothing but dust and ashes, ventured to speak to God on this matter.* Abraham had something we don't have today: It's called reverence. He understood to whom he was talking. Today people don't understand to whom they're talking, when they talk to God. I've heard some say, "Well, you know, I'm not afraid of God." I start backing up, because when the ground opens up under them I don't want to be standing too close. God is an awesome God and He's not to be toyed with. But we don't seem to reverence anyone or anything anymore.

2. *He used a figure that was too high.* So Abraham lowered his number, and Abraham and God continued to bargain. What about forty-five? What about forty? What about thirty or twenty or ten? God said, "I will not destroy it on account of the ten." When Abraham finished bargaining, the LORD departed and Abraham went back to his camp.

In Genesis 19, the story shifts from Abraham and the LORD to the two men who accompanied the LORD. Our previous speculation on the identity of the two men is confirmed: Genesis 19:1 calls them angels. As the two angels approached Sodom in the evening, Lot was sitting in the gate. This implies that Lot was an important man and a leader in Sodom, since the city gates were where the leaders would sit to govern Near Eastern cities.

When Lot saw the two angels he—as his Uncle Abraham had done—extended to them the customary greetings and hospitality of that time. He invited them to stay with him for the night. The angels wanted to stay in the town square, but Lot strongly urged them to stay with him, and he prepared a feast for them.

Before Lot and his guests retired for the evening, the men of Sodom surrounded Lot's house and demanded that he bring out the two men so that they could have homosexual relations with them.

Now we begin to get a picture of the city that Lot had chosen for a home. Remember, Lot chose to go the way of the world when he chose to live there. We also get a glimpse of what the LORD meant when he said that the sin of Sodom was exceedingly grave. Did you know that we get the word *sodomy* from this story about Sodom? Homosexuality is, according to God's Word, an abomination in His sight.

Lot, feeling responsible for his guests, offered these wicked men his two daughters instead. This seems strange to us but may actually have been considered the height of politeness in Lot's culture. Even so, Lot's Middle Eastern morality and sensibilities were not to be substituted for the protection of Jehovah God. So perhaps we get a glimpse of another reason why God separated Lot from Abraham.

> But they said, "Stand aside." Furthermore, they said, "This one came in as an alien, and already he is acting like a judge; now we will treat you worse than them." So they pressed hard against Lot and came near to break the door. (Genesis 19:9)

At this point, the two angels pulled Lot into the house, shut the door, and smote the men with blindness, so that they had trouble finding the door.

Then the angels asked Lot, "Who else do you have in this city? You'd better get them to your house quick, because we're about to destroy this city." This was as serious as it gets. Lot went to plead with his sons-in-law, but to them he appeared to be jesting.

Isn't this the same today? We are concerned about the destruction that will take place before the Second Coming of the LORD, so we go to our relatives to warn them. But they think we are jesting!

Remember, all of this is happening to Lot because of his choices: 1) to leave with Abraham and 2) to dwell in Sodom and Gomorrah. So often we blame the world or the devil or even God for our problems, when it is our own choices that bring us trouble.

When the morning dawned, the angels told Lot to take his wife and two daughters and flee because they were going to destroy the city. Remember, God had agreed to spare the city if ten righteous people could be found in it. But Lot could only come up with four.

It's interesting to me that Peter called Lot *righteous* even though living in Sodom had negatively impacted his values and morality (see 2 Peter 2:7). I believe this is where a number of Christian people are today: They are righteous, meaning they have received the imputed righteousness of Jesus Christ and are attempting to live righteous lives according the power of the Holy Spirit, but they have been greatly impacted by the evil of American culture. They don't even realize how much they have been impacted. Consequently, many of us don't realize how deeply we have been influenced by American culture.

- *We have little passion for the things of God.* If we were passionate about godly things, we'd be on fire about reading His Word, praying, coming to church, witnessing, and obeying God. But, so often we just go through the motions.

- *We have little commitment.* Any old thing will knock us out. "I don't like where they seated me last Sunday, so I'm not going back." "I don't like the songs they sang last time. I'm not going back."

- *We have little submission to either God's direct authority or His delegated authority.* There is no authority over you except what has been established by God. Your husband is a delegated authority. Your mother and father are delegated authorities. The state is a delegated authority. Your pastor is a delegated authority.

- *We have a hard time hearing the voice of God.* People say to me, "I just can't hear God's voice; would you help me make this decision?" You're not going to hear His voice if you don't come to church, read His Word, fellowship with Christians, or pray.

- *We are burned out when we ought to be energized by the power of the Holy Spirit.* Most of the folks I know are burned out. Many are so burned out that they can't get anything, don't know anything, can hardly go on, and can hardly make it. We ought to be empowered by God's Spirit.

When the angels warned Lot to flee, he and his family hesitated. That's understandable. All that they owned and almost everyone they knew were about to be destroyed. But there's another possible reason for their hesitancy: It's possible that they didn't want to leave Sodom because of their attachment to the secularization and sin of the city. God used family mess to get Lot away from Abraham, and He would have to use tragedy to get Lot away from his worldly associations.

God is saying to us, "I want to bless you and give you a destiny, but you will have to leave the comfort, association, and trust in your favorite relatives and you will have to leave your worldly associations and possessions behind."

When Lot and his family hesitated, the angels seized their hands and led them outside of the city, because *God's compassion was upon Lot.* God's compassion was upon Lot even in the midst of family mess and tragedy. God's compassion is upon you, too, even in the midst of family mess and tragedy. This is a great reason to thank and praise God!

In Peter's second letter, he used this situation with Lot to show that God will rescue the godly from temptation. Just as God knew how to rescue Lot from Sodom, where he was oppressed by the sensual conduct of unprincipled men and his soul was tormented by their lawless deeds, He will deliver you from similar godless situations—even if He has to use tragedy that's brought about by your own choices.

After the angels led Lot and his family out of the city, one of them gave this warning: "Escape for your life! Do not look behind you, and do not stay anywhere in the valley; escape to the mountains, or you will be swept away" (Genesis 19:17).

You would think by now, after all that he had seen, Lot would have run away from Sodom as fast as he could. But he didn't. Instead, Lot pleaded with the angels to let him escape to the little town of Zoar. He seemed to be saying, "I can't live in the mountains, far away from Sodom. Let me flee to this little town instead." His life was wrapped up in the whole region of Sodom.

The angels granted Lot's request and urged his speedy escape because they couldn't do anything until he was a safe distance from the coming destruction.

Oh, the truth here is rich! Lot represents those of us who are righteous, but worldly or carnal. John wrote:

> Do not love the world nor the things in the world. If anyone loves the world, the love of the Father is not in him. For all that is in the world, the lust of the flesh and the lust of the eyes and the boastful pride of life, is not from the Father, but is from the world. The world is

passing away, and also its lusts; but the one who does the will of God lives forever. (1 John 2:15–17)

Many times we are just like Lot. God wants to separate us from the world, which often torments us. Yet in spite of the torment, we are so wrapped up, tangled up, and tied up with the world that we feel we can't live without it. We don't believe we can live without the secular associations and possessions of this world—things like worldly friends, TV, movies, and questionable amusements like nightclubs. God is telling us to flee for our lives, but we are still hanging around.

Let's look at television. Do you doubt that television is full of godlessness? Sometimes God wants us to put it away for a while—maybe a day, a week, or maybe forever. You'd think that when people got saved they'd run for their lives from the godless things that they see on TV. God is saying, "Flee for your life, run!" And, we say, "I want to run, but can I just see my favorite program first?"

What about movies? There are some churches and groups in this country that don't allow people in leadership positions to go to the movies. I'm not saying that's right or wrong, I'm saying it's at least a standard. Where are our standards today? We'll watch anything, and then wonder why we are the way we are. God is telling us, "Flee for your life!"

Not only are we tormented, but we're also tempted—and God wants to deliver us from both. He sends his angels to lead us *by the hand* out of temptation. But, even after He has led us out, we stand around and ask God if we can remain close to the secular, sinful lifestyle that we have grown accustomed to. God, being the compassionate God that He is, often grants our requests. But there is a price to pay.

When Lot reached Zoar, the Lord rained fire and brimstone on Sodom and Gomorrah. "Brimstone" means burning sulfur. I am told that sulfur is one of the residues left after a nuclear blast. This indicates that God destroyed Sodom and Gomorrah with fire and tremendous heat. He wiped out both people and the vegetation.

One day God will begin His urban renewal project on earth.

> But the day of the Lord will come like a thief, in which the heavens will pass away with a roar and the elements will be destroyed with intense heat, and the earth and its works will be burned up. Since all these things are to be destroyed in this way, what sort of people ought you to be in holy conduct and godliness, looking for and hastening the coming of the day of God, because of which the heavens will be destroyed by burning, and the elements will melt with intense heat! But according to His promise we are looking for new heavens and a new earth, in which righteousness dwells. (2 Peter 3:10–13)

It behooves us to be ready by living a life of godliness through the power of the Holy Spirit.

In Genesis 19:26, we are given—in just one verse—some very shocking and important information about Lot's wife: "But his wife, from behind him, looked back, and she became a pillar of salt." I'll talk more about this action and its impact upon her daughters, in the next chapter. For now, let's continue our look at Abraham's journey.

Abraham rose early in the morning, as many men of God were known to do in that day, and stood in the place where he had stood before the Lord. As he stood there, looking toward Sodom and Gomorrah and the valley where these two cities were situated, he beheld smoke rising from the land like smoke rising from a furnace. We clearly see

Abraham's continued impact upon Lot's life: when God destroyed the cities of Sodom and Gomorrah, He remembered Abraham and sent Lot out of the midst of those cities.

- God remembered Abraham.
- He remembered His covenant with Abraham.
- He remembered His promise and destiny for Abraham.
- He remembered Abraham's pleading and praying for Lot.

Because of one righteous man, God rescued Lot from the midst of Sodom and Gomorrah and did not destroy him.

Even though God may separate you from some of your relatives for a greater purpose and your fellowship with them is almost nonexistent, don't forget about them. Intercede for them through strong, persistent prayer. Plead and bargain for their lives. Perhaps God will deliver your relatives because of you.

I've seen God deliver people out of impossible situations. I've seen people who were far from home, tied up in dope, caught up with hustlers and gangs. Some said these people couldn't be redeemed or set free, but I've seen God send angels in among violent people, grab them by the hand and lead them out.

Keep praying for your friends and relatives down in Sodom and Gomorrah. God might just deliver them on account of you.

Discussion Questions

1. Can you think of any relatives whom God has separated from you who need your continued intercessory prayer?

2. Can you relate to Lot's entanglement with his culture? On a scale of 1 to 10, with 1 being no impact and 10 being totally overwhelmed, rate your present entanglement in your culture. How would someone who knows you well rate you?

3. Devise and share your plan to intercede for separated family members that are living in Sodom and Gomorrah.

Chapter Five

In the Grip of a Mother's Gaze
(One Life to Live)

The angels had just led Lot, his wife and two daughters out of Sodom. They were fleeing for their lives because God was about to destroy the wicked cities of that well-watered valley.

Let's pick up the story in Genesis 19:23–38.

> The sun had risen over the earth when Lot came to Zoar. Then the LORD rained on Sodom and Gomorrah brimstone and fire from the LORD out of heaven, and He overthrew those cities, and all the valley, and all the inhabitants of the cities, and what grew on the ground. But his wife, from behind him, looked back, and she became a pillar of salt.

> Now Abraham arose early in the morning and went to the place where he had stood before the LORD; and he looked down toward Sodom and Gomorrah, and toward all the land of the valley, and he saw, and behold, the smoke of the land ascended like the smoke of a furnace.

> Thus it came about, when God destroyed the cities of the valley, that God remembered Abraham, and sent Lot out of the midst of the overthrow, when He overthrew the cities in which Lot lived. (Genesis 19:23–29)

When Lot and his family reached Zoar, God destroyed Sodom and Gomorrah. This is a picture of what will happen at the end of the world as we know it. When we, God's children, the elect of all the ages, are safe—i.e., after the rapture or translation—God is going to destroy this world with fervent heat.

The cultural conditions in Sodom also approximate the cultural conditions that will exist when Jesus is revealed in His Second Coming and the world is destroyed; as well as the cultural conditions during the time of Noah, when the world was destroyed by the flood.

In the New Testament it says,

> And just as it happened in the days of Noah, so it will be also in the days of the Son of Man: they were eating, they were drinking, they were marrying, they were being given in marriage, until the day that Noah entered the ark, and the flood came and destroyed them all.

> It was the same as happened in the days of Lot: they were eating, they were drinking, they were buying, they were selling, they were planting, they were building; but on the day that Lot went out from Sodom it rained fire and brimstone from heaven and destroyed them all.

> It will be just the same on the day that the Son of Man is revealed. (Luke 17:26–30)

Aren't we experiencing the same cultural conditions now?

- *Aren't people eating as never before?* There are restaurants everywhere and more are being built. It's a drive-through generation. Doesn't anybody cook anymore?

- *Aren't people drinking as never before?* There are more beverages, alcoholic and non-alcoholic, to choose from today than there have ever been in the history of man.

- *Aren't people marrying and being given in marriage as never before?* Marrying, divorcing, and remarrying. With many divorced people getting remarried six and seven times, it makes the marriage rate go up.

- *Aren't people buying as never before?* Consumerism is at an all-time high. For those of us who are just plain lazy, we don't have to go grocery shopping anymore. We can go online with our computers, order our groceries and they will bring them to our homes.

- *Aren't people selling as never before?*

- Aren't fewer farmers planting than ever before?

- *Aren't people building as never before?* There are new, much larger, expensive houses continually going up all around Akron, Ohio, where I live.

The conditions are perfect for the return of Jesus Christ!

Returning to the family mess saga, we now come to an important editorial comment, in verse 26: "But his wife, from behind him, looked back, and she became a pillar of salt" (Genesis 19:26).

We don't even get this poor woman's name, but we do get a summation of her actions and their consequences. The phrase *looked back* in Hebrew is *nabat*. It means "to scan or look intently at." By implication it means "to regard with pleasure, favor, or care."[1]

Lot's wife didn't glance back casually on Sodom and Gomorrah and the destruction that was taking place. She gazed back with pleasure. She was fondly remembering a city that was totally vile, evil, corrupt, and against God. She was enamored with Sodom and did not want to leave it, or have it destroyed. She loved Sodom and Gomorrah. She loved the world. Therefore, the love of the Father was not in her (1 John 2:15).

I believe that Jesus touched on this situation in Luke's Gospel:

> Another also said, "I will follow You, Lord; but first permit me to say good-bye to those at home." But Jesus said to him, "No one, after putting his hand to the plow and looking back, is fit for the kingdom of God." (Luke 9:61–62)

You can't plow a straight row while looking back. The only way to plow straight is to keep your eyes straight ahead. He that keeps intently looking back will plow crookedly.

I believe Jesus is talking about discipleship here. In the preceding verses He said, "Follow Me!" No one can plow a straight row as a disciple by longingly looking back to a past life or love. Jesus lets us know that this applies to something much more than plowing in a field. He who puts his hand to the plow and looks back is not fit for the kingdom of God. The Greek word behind *fit* is *euthetos,* which means "well-placed, suited for, or adapted to."[2]

A person who intently and longingly looks back upon his past life has not adapted to and is not suited for kingdom life. Such a person is not suited because of worldly impulses and passions (the impulses and passions have not been adapted to the kingdom life); "not suited with regard to conflicting duties" (a disciple's duties are before her, towards heaven, not behind her in the past and the world) and, "not suited for the kingdom of heaven, from the perspective of a divided mind" (her mind is divided from the things of God and His kingdom).

Doesn't this describe many Christians today? They have placed their faith in Jesus Christ for salvation, but:

- They are looking back into the world.
- Their impulses and passions are worldly.
- They are conflicted about their duties.
- Their minds are divided.

Instead of looking to the future and the new city and destiny where God is leading, they are looking intently and longingly towards the city where they used to live. They are rehearsing with fondness the evil, vile, godless city and lovingly remembering their past life in sin.

What is the consequence of looking back? Lot's wife turned into a pillar of salt.

To me, Lot represents something quite different than his wife and family. He was called righteous, but no one else in his family was. Even though Lot was righteous, he had become so entangled in the culture of Sodom that he was saved on the basis of Abraham—not because of his own righteousness whereas Lot's family was saved because of Lot.

Lot's wife was saved from the destruction of Sodom and Gomorrah, but she was turned into a pillar of salt when she looked back. Salt symbolizes many things in the Bible, but in this case I believe it is a symbol of desolation and barrenness, which represents the barrenness of the Dead Sea, i.e., the biblical Salt Sea.

Lot's wife escaped destruction, but her life ended up in desolation and barrenness. She had but "One Life to Live." Wouldn't it have been better had she lived it for God?

It's the same for some Christians: Many of us are dead and barren because we've got an inlet but no outlet. We come to church and take in, but we never let out. We come to church and eat and eat, but we're not serving in any ministry, or we're not ministering to anybody on a regular basis. What happens? We die! Nothing can live in us because we are barren, like the Dead Sea.

- We can escape Sodom and Gomorrah and still end up desolate and barren.
- We can escape fire and brimstone and still end up with a life that is desolate and barren of impact.
- We can escape the lake that burns with fire and brimstone and still experience desolation and barrenness in this life, which will cause us to lose our reward in the life to come, and result in weeping and gnashing of teeth when we see Him.

This leads me to Lot's two daughters, who were caught in the grip of their mother's gaze. Their mother gazed back upon Sodom and that gaze had a profound impact upon her two daughters. Soon after this, Lot's two daughters committed incest with him to preserve their family line. As we say colloquially, "What a mess!"

> Lot went up from Zoar, and stayed in the mountains, and his two daughters with him; for he was afraid to stay in Zoar; and he stayed in a cave, he and his two daughters.

Then the firstborn said to the younger, "Our father is old, and there is not a man on earth to come in to us after the manner of the earth. Come, let us make our father drink wine, and let us lie with him that we may preserve our family through our father." So they made their father drink wine that night, and the firstborn went in and lay with her father; and he did not know when she lay down or when she arose.

On the following day, the firstborn said to the younger, "Behold, I lay last night with my father; let us make him drink wine tonight also; then you go in and lie with him, that we may preserve our family through our father." So they made their father drink wine that night also, and the younger arose and lay with him; and he did not know when she lay down or when she arose.

Thus both the daughters of Lot were with child by their father. The firstborn bore a son, and called his name Moab; he is the father of the Moabites to this day. As for the younger, she also bore a son, and called his name Ben-ammi; he is the father of the sons of Ammon to this day. (Genesis 19:30–38)

We don't know about the family mess of Lot's wife, but there must have been some because she left a terrible family legacy to her daughters. Whatever family mess she experienced in the past culminated in her looking longingly back at Sodom.

- That look had an impact upon her daughters.
- That look taught her daughters something about their mother's values.
- That look confirmed some values for her daughters.

- That look continued her daughters' entanglement into the culture and values of Sodom.

- That look taught her daughters something about what they should love.

- That look confirmed negative conclusions about past family mess in her daughters.

- That look clouded the future for her daughters.

- That look taught her daughters that sin was more desirable than righteousness.

- That look became a trap to her daughters.

These two daughters were trapped in the grip of their mother's gaze.

If you're a mother, beware of your gaze! Be careful what you gaze upon, because your daughters may be trapped in the grip of your gaze. Until now we've been mostly talking about the sin of the fathers, but the Bible says the sin of the mothers impacts future generations, too. Your daughters will be caught in the grip of whatever you gaze upon. If your gaze is toward the way of the world, that grip may manifest itself in the following ways (by the way, these also apply to sons):

1. *Gazing back at Sodom may teach your daughters to love the world rather than the things of God.* What do they see in you? What will be emblazoned into their minds about you as their mother? If they saw you gazing back with fondness, they will learn to love the world rather than the things of God.

2. *Gazing back at Sodom may teach your daughters to be enamored with sin rather than with holy living.* If they

saw you enamored with sin, constantly gazing back at it after your salvation, and the barrenness in your life because of that fixation, don't think that your daughters will escape that. God may save them and they may move on, but don't think that they can escape the impact of your gaze. They may even become trapped by it.

3. *Gazing back at Sodom may teach your daughters to live in the past rather than living in the present and looking toward the future.* Many people blame everything that's wrong with them on the fact that their mothers didn't give them enough milk and cookies or whatever. You can't always live in the past. You've got to take responsibility for your own life and your own choices. It's time to be running for your life, not looking back at yesteryear.

4. *Gazing back at Sodom may teach your daughters to be trapped in the evil of their past.* Some people have had truly horrible things done to them, and I have great compassion for them. But, if you constantly look back at that you can become trapped by it. If you don't deal with these tragedies, your daughters may become trapped by them, too. They'll be trapped by a legacy of evil that happened to you and may be left trying to finish up your pain.

5. *Gazing back at Sodom may teach your daughters to love the culture rather than the principles of the Word of God.* When we're fixated on the ways of the world, we care less about the principles of God. Instead of becoming biblically astute we become politically correct. We can't talk about abortion anymore because people will get mad at us. We can't talk about divorce anymore because folks will be upset. We look at life from a cultural perspective, not a biblical one. Brother or sister, it doesn't

matter what the TV says about abortion or divorce or whatever; what matters is what the Bible says about it.

6. *Gazing back at Sodom may teach your daughters something abnormal and abominable about human sexuality.* What have your daughters seen about your own sexuality? Most of us have never seen or learned much about our parents' sexuality, because they hid it from us. Don't misunderstand me: parents should hide the actual act of intercourse from their children, but I don't believe they should hide sensuality from them. Because we can't learn about *normal* family, love, affection, intimacy, sensuality, sexuality, and relationships, if we don't see and experience it—in healthy ways—in our own families. But what did your daughters see? Have they seen you let men stay overnight?

7. *Gazing back at Sodom may teach your daughters something perverted about their womanhood.* The reason we don't have many real, biblical women today is that many of our females are looking back at the culture to learn how to be a woman. You shouldn't look at soap operas to learn how to be a woman. Don't look at TV programs to figure out how a woman is supposed to live. Look in the Word of God to find out what God wants a woman to be.

8. *Gazing back at Sodom may teach your daughters to dishonor their parents.* Think about Lot's daughters' conspiracy to commit incest with him. How much honor did they show him when they tricked him into having sex with them, not once, but twice? Family mess and parental dishonor are the legacy of Lot's wife.

9. *Gazing back at Sodom may teach your daughters to have messy, sinful ideas about how to fulfill their destiny.* Again,

think about Lot's daughters committing incest. What a mess. You don't fulfill your destiny by sin; you fulfill your destiny through God. They said, "We're not going to have any offspring, so we've got to do something about it." What about waiting on the LORD? They took matters into their own hands and created a big-time family mess.

A lot of this reminds me of a later prophecy of Ezekiel:

> Behold, everyone who quotes proverbs will quote this proverb concerning you, saying, "Like mother, like daughter!"' (Ezekiel 16:44)

I want to wrap up this chapter with two observations.

Observation #1—Illustrating the phrase "visiting the iniquity of the fathers upon the children to the third and fourth generations," we have looked at the impact of family mess in two generations. Lot was undoubtedly impacted by his father Haran, who is Abraham's brother. And Lot's daughters were impacted by Lot and his wife.

Observation #2—We see that God worked beneath, behind, through, above, and beyond family mess. God worked in spite of the family mess to deliver Lot and his daughters from destruction down in Sodom.

Our God is a compassionate and powerful God! He will work beneath, behind, through, above, beyond, and in spite of family mess to deliver us, His children, from destruction and to our destiny!

Discussion Questions

1. Can you detect any evidence that you are entangled in the grip of your mother's gaze?

2. How do you plan to fight that entanglement?

3. Is there anything in your life that has the focus of your attention more than God?

4. If you suspect that your answer to the previous question is yes, what impact might that gaze have upon your children?

5. What kind of legacy do you want to leave for your children? How are you making that happen today?

1. *Strong's Greek and Hebrew Dictionary* (Database c. 1990–93 NavPress Software).

2. A.T. Robertson, *Word Pictures in the Greek New Testament*.

Chapter Six

One Wife Too Many
(The Young and the Restless)

We detoured in the land of Sodom and Gomorrah for a few chapters, as we studied Lot and his family. Now we return to our exploration of Abraham and his immediate family line, to see how God worked beneath, behind, through, above, and beyond his family mess.

Even though there was a lot of family mess going on in Abraham's immediate family, I want you to notice something: God did not hesitate to proclaim Himself the God of Abraham, Isaac, and Jacob. God did not run from the mess of this family. On the contrary, He identified Himself as the God of this family. Isn't that encouraging for you in your family mess? God will not run from you just because you've got a mess on your hands.

Now we come to the third major mess of Abraham's family.

- The first mess had to do with Abraham leaving Babylonia and his father's house.

- The second mess had to do with God separating Lot from Abraham.
- The third mess has to do with Abraham's wife.

Let's look at Genesis 16:

Now Sarai, Abram's wife had borne him no children, and she had an Egyptian maid whose name was Hagar. So Sarai said to Abram, "Now behold, the LORD has prevented me from bearing children. Please go in to my maid; perhaps I will obtain children through her." And Abram listened to the voice of Sarai.

After Abram had lived ten years in the land of Canaan, Abram's wife Sarai took Hagar the Egyptian, her maid, and gave her to her husband Abram as his wife. He went in to Hagar, and she conceived; and when she saw that she had conceived, her mistress was despised in her sight. And Sarai said to Abram, "May the wrong done me be upon you. I gave my maid into your arms, but when she saw that she had conceived, I was despised in her sight. May the LORD judge between you and me."

But Abram said to Sarai, "Behold, your maid is in your power; do to her what is good in your sight." So Sarai treated her harshly, and she fled from her presence.

Now the angel of the LORD found her by a spring of water in the wilderness, by the spring on the way to Shur. He said, "Hagar, Sarai's maid, where have you come from and where are you going?" And she said, "I am fleeing from the presence of my mistress Sarai." Then the angel of the LORD said to her, "Return to your mistress, and submit yourself to her authority." Moreover, the angel of the LORD said to her, "I will greatly multiply your descendants so that they will be too many to count."

The angel of the LORD said to her further, "Behold, you are with child, And you will bear a son; And you shall call his name Ishmael, Because the LORD has given heed to your affliction. He will be a wild donkey of a man, His hand will be against everyone, And everyone's hand will be against him; And he will live to the east of all his brothers."

Then she called the name of the LORD who spoke to her, "You are a God who sees"; for she said, "Have I even remained alive here after seeing Him?" Therefore the well was called Beer-lahai-roi; behold, it is between Kadesh and Bered. (Genesis 16:1–14)

Here Sarah is still called Sarai and Abraham is still called Abram, but for convenience, we will call them Sarah and Abraham.

The lack of children, particularly a male heir, was one of the most formidable problems of Abraham's life. God had given Abraham a tremendous promise of making a great nation out of him, through a son who would be his heir. God had told Abraham that his descendents would be as numerous as the stars of heaven and the grains of sand on the seashores of the world, which, by the way, are roughly equivalent of 10^{18}. That's a tremendous amount. Consequently, Abraham had trouble believing these promises of God, because he and his wife were old and past the child-bearing years.

Sarah had borne Abraham no children. To her, this was the curse of God. Sarah believed that God had prevented her from having children. To fully understand this passage of Scripture, you will need to know something about the culture and prevailing norms of that period.

Women during that time believed that children were a gift from the LORD. The more children they had, the more favor they believed they had in God's eyes. They also believed, conversely, that if they had no children God had cursed them. So children were of prime importance to women of that time. This is in stark contrast to today, when many believe that children are a curse and that the fewer you have the more blessed you are!

Armed with this understanding, we can relate to Sarah. She had to do something about her childlessness. Sarah was one of "The Young and the Restless." She couldn't trust in or wait upon the promise of God. It didn't seem to dawn on her to pray, instead she offers Abraham her personal servant as a concubine or surrogate wife and mother.

Before you judge Sarah too harshly, understand that this was probably the custom of people of the day. But it doesn't matter that this was the custom of the world: was it the plan of God? The answer is *no!* How do I know? Because I've read through the Bible approximately thirty times. I know what God's will and plan for marriage entails, and His will and plan is one man for one woman for a lifetime.

Genesis 2:24 says, "For this reason a man shall leave his father and his mother, and be joined to his wife; and they shall become one flesh." And Mark 10:9 tops it off: "What therefore God has joined together, let no man separate."

In the case of Adam and Eve, they were the only two people on earth. In time they had children, but these children were ineligible for marriage. So it's clear from God's Word and the circumstances that it was His will for Adam and Eve to have one mate for their lifetime.

We have something that Adam and Eve didn't have: a completed canon or set of books of the Word of God. When you read the Word of God, you will see that He allowed remarriage in the case of death. Preachers and scholars

86

So, what did Abraham do? He did what he normally did: nothing. He didn't confront his first wife or protect the rights of his second wife and coming child. Instead, he allowed Sarah to do whatever she wanted to do. Abraham, in my opinion, was a passive man who had trouble trusting God. But God was making him into a man of courage and faith, in spite of his family mess.

When you read in the New Testament that Abraham is called the father of faith, don't attribute that to Abraham's natural ability. Attribute it to God working supremely and sovereignly in his life to make him into something that would last throughout eternity—in spite of the family mess. It should cause you to praise God when you realize there was no way in the world that Abraham, on his own, could become the father of faith. He was weak in his flesh and he had formidable family mess, but still God made him into something great. That should give you hope.

When Sarah saw Hagar's new attitude, she treated Hagar harshly, and Hagar ran from her presence. Two women couldn't live in the same tent then, and the same is true today.

Now the angel of the LORD found Hagar and spoke to her. I believe this is another pre-incarnate appearance of Christ. He told her to go back to Sarah and submit to her authority—a strange bit of advice. Not many modern Christians want to understand it, much less live it out. Yet God's answer to the situation was to go back and experience the pain, because He had something He wanted to do for Hagar in the midst of her family mess.

No, God didn't tell her to find her own apartment, file for legal separation, or sue for a divorce. He told her to be an adult. Adulthood is the ability to face the reality of your situation and have the courage to make the best of it,

disagree over the various conditions of remarriage, but let's agree that at a minimum God intended one man for one woman at a time. So, Sarah's offer was not in keeping with God's will and plan.

We also know that it was not God's will for Abraham to have a child through his wife's handmaid, because God had given him a promise about his own children through Sarah. Nevertheless, Abraham listened to the voice of his wife instead of the voice of God.

Once again we see Abraham's difficulty in trusting Jehovah God. Once again we see his difficulty in assertively confronting one of his relatives. Once again we see that it leads to family mess. He could not confront Lot about leaving Babylon with him, and he did not confront his wife about her offer. We have no way of knowing, but it seems reasonable to assume that this offer also appealed to Abraham's flesh. Be that as it may, family mess began when Abraham listened to his wife instead of trusting in the promise of God.

This was Adam's problem, too. If we go back to the Garden of Eden, we find that listed as the major reason Adam was about to experience the consequences of sin.

> Then to Adam He said, "Because you have listened to the voice of your wife, and have eaten from the tree about which I commanded you, saying, 'You shall not eat from it'; cursed is the ground because of you; in toil you will eat of it all the days of your life. Both thorns and thistles it shall grow for you; and you will eat the plants of the field; by the sweat of your face you will eat bread, till you return to the ground, because from it you were taken; for you are dust, and to dust you shall return." (Genesis 3:17–19)

Family mess entered the world when Adam listened to his wife instead of trusting in God, and that same family mess is playing itself out in the narrative before us.

If you're a husband, there will come a time when your wife will offer you an alternative to the command and will of God. Your response to that offer will determine the intensity of the family mess that you will experience and pass on to your posterity.

• You must obey God rather than Humanity.

• You must obey God's Word rather than your wife.

• You must do all that you can to please your wife, but God's Word has to come first.

So Abraham went into Sarah's handmaid, Hagar, and she conceived. This was certainly a fall, like Adam's, and it seems to relate to the first fall.

Husband, when your wife struggles against you and offers you an alternative to the will of God, don't accept it. If you do, you will encounter family mess and she will lose respect for you. You must treat her with love, but you have to stand your ground. Now, that can be a hard thing to do. Most of us men can treat our wives with love but we can't hold our ground. Some of us can hold our ground but we can't treat our wives with love. We have to do both.

When Abraham went into Hagar, he started something that plagued the children of Israel for thousands of years: polygamy, the practice of having more than one wife. The cultures around Abraham practiced polygamy freely, but this is the first reference to it among God's chosen people. The family mess that Abraham planted that day would bear fruit and become one of the causes of the nation of Israel going into captivity.

Hundreds of years later we see Solomon with his three hundred wives and seven hundred concubines. A thousand women! These were not just regular marriages, but political alliances with the nations of the earth. The Bible tells us that these foreign women turned Solomon's heart away from God. God then allowed the kingdom to break up and, ultimately, the Israelites to go into captivity. Remember how that got started: Abraham, Sarah, and Hagar.

When Hagar saw that she was pregnant, she despised her mistress. She now had something Sarah didn't have. She also shared something with Abraham that he and Sarah didn't share. It appeared that Hagar had God's blessing and that Sarah was cursed.

The family mess increased when Abraham had to deal with two wives instead of one, *and* a child on the way. Abraham had one wife too many. It has been said that a man is too much man for one woman but not enough man for two women, so we have to settle for one. If Abraham had trouble dealing with one wife, he would have double trouble dealing with two.

Perhaps the main potential for devastating family mess was Abraham's temptation to use Ishmael—his son [by] Hagar—as his heir, instead of waiting upon God's prom[ise]. Satan wanted Abraham to settle for second best, [in]stead of the divine blessing that God wanted to best[ow.] Satan wants all men of God to settle for second best, ra[ther] than experience the divine blessing, promise, and de[stiny] that God has in store for them. Husband, Satan mig[ht want] to use your wife to trick you out of receiving the pr[omise] of God. Be on guard.

Abraham had constant turmoil in his home bec[ause of] these two wives. Sarah's plan to ingratiate hersel[f to her] husband backfired, and when she saw that Hagar [despised] her, she complained to Abraham.

through the power of the Holy Spirit. Sometimes God works in the midst of family mess.

I want to make it clear that I'm not telling anyone to stay in an abusive situation. I'm merely pointing out that we all have some messy situations that we want to run from. Some of them we should avoid, but we should first seek God to find out which are which. There are some messy situations that God wants to deliver us from, and there are some messy situations that God wants to take us through.

God went on to tell Hagar what He was going to do for her, right in Abraham's house, right before her enemy Sarah. This reminds me of the words of David in Psalm 23: "Thou preparest a table before me in the presence of mine enemies: thou anointest my head with oil; my cup runneth over" (Psalm 23:5, KJV). When God wants to give you a promise and a blessing, no enemy or family mess can thwart Him.

He promised Hagar two things:

- *I will greatly multiply your descendents so that they will be too many to count.* Now she would really be considered blessed, and not by her own hands.

- *I will give you a son.* Children were considered a blessing of God, but a son was a special blessing because the family line was carried on through the son.

Our first response to affliction naturally is to try to get out of it. But, sometimes, our family mess is a conduit through which God wants to give us a promise and a blessing. *God doesn't always move the mountain; sometimes He gives us the strength to climb it.*

We said before that God sometimes separates us from family mess. Yes, He does! But I have to tell you that sometimes

He sends us right back into it—not just back into it, but back into it to submit to someone's authority. That's not much fun, is it? No, but sometimes it's God's way.

Here we see that Abraham's family mess resulted in even more family mess. God told Hagar that Ishmael would be a wild donkey of a man who would be against everyone and whom everyone would be against. He would live to the east of the Israelites. As we've seen, living and traveling east seemed to imply going the way of the world as opposed to the way of God. Hagar would give birth to another nation of enemies against Israel. Later, in Genesis 37:25, Joseph would be sold to Ishmaelites. And this people group became the Arab Nations, who are still Israel's enemies today.

Even though His blessing will result in more enemies against His chosen people, God has compassion on Hagar and blesses her. So Hagar calls God "the God who sees me" (Genesis 16:13b, NIV). She recognized the compassion of God in watching over her and letting her live. Our God is a God who sees us!

- He sees us in our most desperate hour.
- He has His all-seeing eye on us.
- We are the apple of His eye.
- We are the pupil, the most tender portion, of His eye.
- He is watching over us.
- He knows just how much we can bear.

Paul spoke to this:

No temptation has overtaken you but such as is common to man; and God is faithful, who will not allow you to be tempted beyond what you are able, but with the temptation will provide the way of escape also, so that you will be able to endure it. (1 Corinthians 10:13)

As the curtain drops on this narrative, we're given information about Abraham's age. Why? Because it helps us to better understand the impact of family mess. He was 86 when Ishmael was born. In chapter 21 we find out that he was 100 when Isaac was born. It may be that Sarah's idea to bear a child through Hagar actually delayed the promise of God for fourteen years.

Nevertheless, God, being the compassionate God that He is, eventually blessed Sarah with a son—one who would be in the line of the coming Messiah. God is the God of Abraham, Abraham's son (Isaac), and Abraham's grandson (Jacob). Can you believe that God works beneath, behind, through, above, and beyond family mess?

There are several important lessons that we should learn here:

- *God's promises and plans cannot be stopped by family mess.* What God wants to do in your life cannot be stopped by family mess. It can be stopped by your sin, but not by family mess.

- *God's promises and plans can be delayed by family mess.* Sometimes what God wants to do He delays because of the mess that's going on.

- Family mess is very messy and painful.

- Family mess breeds more family mess.

- *If we want to hasten our rise above family sin and family mess, we must not be "Young and Restless."* We must be mature, trusting, and patient. When God is ready, it will come. There's no use in creating family mess to try to hurry God, because we'll only slow down the promises.

- *If we want to hasten our rise above family sin and family mess, we must accept God's vision for our posterity.* Sarah was unwilling to accept God's vision. She had her own plan. She probably thought, "You aren't moving, LORD, and I don't know what You're going to do, I don't have any children, so I'm going to give Hagar to Abraham." She took matters into her own hands, and look at what happened! We must learn to accept God's vision for our posterity.

- *If we want to hasten our rise above family sin and family mess, we must trust God's vision for our posterity.* We must not only accept it, but trust it.

Discussion Questions

1. Are there any situations in your life in which someone is offering you a shortcut to the plan of God?

2. Are you a get-it-done-myself kind of person or a wait-for-the-will-of-God kind of person? Justify your answer.

3. On a scale of 1 to 10, with 1 being the lowest and 10 being the highest, rate your maturity, your trust in God, and your patience with God's plan. Please explain each rating.

4. In what ways might family mess delay your possession of God's blessing and destiny for your life?

5. In what ways is God making you aware of His destiny for you, in spite of family mess?

Chapter Seven

In the Image of Your Father
(One Life to Live)

We've looked at how Sarah and Abraham tried to hurry God by bearing a son through Hagar and we've seen how that backfired, as family mess so often does. Now let's jump ahead to Isaac, the heir of promise. Because I want to examine him as an adult, let's briefly review what happened between these two stories.

Genesis 21 through 24 tells how God was faithful to His promise and gave Abraham and Sarah a child of their own. These chapters tell the story of Isaac's birth, circumcision, childhood, and the strain caused by the presence of Ishmael, Hagar's son. They explain how God tested Abraham's faith by asking him to sacrifice Isaac, and then prevented him from going through with it. They tell of Sarah's death. And, finally, these chapters recount the story of how Rebekah became Isaac's wife.

Isaac is the second generation after Abraham. We'll now look at the impact of family mess in his life and God's providence in spite of the family mess. Let's begin with a passage from Genesis 26:

> Now there was a famine in the land, besides the previous famine that had occurred in the days of Abraham. So Isaac went to Gerar, to Abimelech king of the Philistines.

> The LORD appeared to him and said, "Do not go down to Egypt; stay in the land of which I shall tell you. Sojourn in this land and I will be with you and bless you, for to you and to your descendants I will give all these lands, and I will establish the oath which I swore to your father Abraham. I will multiply your descendants as the stars of heaven, and will give your descendants all these lands; and by your descendants all the nations of the earth shall be blessed; because Abraham obeyed Me and kept My charge, My commandments, My statutes and My laws." (Genesis 26:1–5)

We come now to an important experience in the life of Isaac, the biological son of Abraham and the heir that God had promised to Abraham and Sarah. It came about that there was a famine in the land. To survive, Isaac went to the Philistine city of Gerar, where Abimelech the king of the Philistines lived. While Isaac was at Gerar, God appeared to him, gave him some instructions, and extended to him the promise He'd given to his father, Abraham. God told Isaac not to go down to Egypt, but to sojourn in the land of the Philistines.

God also said He would do four things for Isaac: "I will be with you; I will bless you; I will give all of these lands to you and your descendants; and I will establish the oath I swore to your father Abraham" (Genesis 26:3). Let's look at these four in order.

First, God promised that *He would always be with Isaac.* What more could Isaac want than the company of God? What more could *we* want than the company of God? In fact, we have more than Isaac had. The Bible says that all three persons of the Trinity—God, Jesus Christ, and the Holy Spirit—dwell within us.

In Matthew 28, Jesus gave the Great Commission:

> Go therefore and make disciples of all the nations, baptizing them in the name of the Father and the Son and the Holy Spirit, teaching them to observe all that I commanded you; and lo, I am with you always, even to the end of the age. (Matthew 28:19–20)

In the Greek, the phrase *I am with you always* literally means "I am with you all days." Jesus is telling us He will be with us during all kinds of days. He will be with us during:

- dark days
- difficult days
- depressing days
- discouraging days
- distracted days
- despairing days

God has promised to be with us in all days. What a promise!

The second thing God promised Isaac was that *He would bless him.* Who else could bless Isaac but Jehovah God, the source of all blessing? Likewise, who else can bless us but God?

As a matter of fact, God has already blessed us. Paul said in Ephesians, "Blessed be the God and Father of our Lord Jesus Christ, who has blessed us with every spiritual blessing in the heavenly places in Christ" (Ephesians 1:3).

These are only a few of the spiritual blessings. God bestows upon us:

- election
- predestination
- regeneration
- redemption
- justification
- divine providence
- glorification

The third promise to Isaac was God's reaffirmation of His oath to give Abraham's descendents the Promised Land: "I . . . will give your descendants all of these lands" (Gen. 26:3–4).

For Christians, the Promised Land is abundant Christian living. Eventually, we'll enter the New Jerusalem. God doesn't want just to save us; He wants to give us the abundant Christian life. Jesus said, "The thief comes only to steal and kill and destroy; I came that they may have life, and have it abundantly" (John 10:10). God promises us this land.

With the fourth promise, God extends to Isaac the promises that He had made to Abraham. The LORD then recounts the particulars of that oath:

1. I will multiply your descendants as the stars of heaven.
2. I will give your descendants all these lands.
3. By your descendants all the nations of the earth shall be blessed.

Among Isaac's descendants are the greatest kings of Israel, including David and Solomon. Isaac's descendants also included Jesus Christ, the coming King of kings. Jesus received His legal right to the throne of David from his adoptive father, Joseph, who was in the line of Isaac. Scholars believe that Mary was also in the line of David, so Jesus got a double dose. All of the nations of the earth, for all time, would be blessed in Jesus Christ.

After reminding him of the promises, God told Isaac why they were still good and extended to him: "because Abraham obeyed Me and kept My charge, My commandments, My statutes and My laws" (Genesis 26:5).

What powerful proof that God works through family mess to bring a man to his destiny! Abraham, whom we've seen struggle with trust in and obedience to God, hears God Himself affirm that he had kept God's commandments, statutes, and laws.

We can now take up the other verses upon which this book is based. Let's return to Exodus 20.

> You shall not worship them or serve them; for I, the LORD your God, am a jealous God, visiting the iniquity of the fathers on the children, on the third and the fourth generations of those who hate Me, *but showing lovingkindness to thousands, to those who love Me and keep My commandments.* (Exodus 20:5–6, emphasis mine)

As I explained in an earlier chapter, the retribution includes punishment for sin and reward for righteousness. It works both ways. God will visit on His people both the consequences of the iniquity of their fathers *and* the lovingkindness demonstrated by fathers who love God and keep His commandments. It was because of Abraham's love of God and obedience that God showed His lovingkindness to Isaac.

We often talk about all the bad things that happen to us because of what our mothers or fathers did wrong. "I'm messed up because my mother never read to me" or "I'm this way because my father never told me he loved me." We feel cursed because of what happened to us in the past. But, have we ever considered that we are *blessed* because of what happened in the past?

Personally, I'm experiencing the consequences of the sins of my forefathers. But I'm also experiencing the lovingkindness of God, because of my forefathers' love of God and obedience to His commandments. My father is a preacher, my grandfather was a preacher, and there are people of faith on both sides of my family. Therefore, it is possible and probable that some of the lovingkindness of God that I am experiencing is the result of my forefathers' godliness.

Here's another comforting thought: It's possible that my children are experiencing the lovingkindness of God as a result of *my* love and obedience to God, as well as that of my forefathers.

The lovingkindness God showed to Abraham lasted all the way to the birth of Jesus Christ and beyond. In Matthew, Mary was overshadowed by the power of the Holy Spirit and a child was placed within her. She then told Elizabeth that this was the promise to Abraham. To Abraham! That's at least forty-two generations away! The promise to Abraham ran through Abraham, Isaac, Jacob, Joseph, and all the way to Jesus Christ.

Love God and obey His commandments for your children's sake, and for the sake of your grandchildren and great-grandchildren! Who knows how far down the line that blessing will be visited? Blessings will come to them because of your faithfulness. How's that for another good reason to love and obey God?

Let's return now to the rest of the story.

> So Isaac lived in Gerar. When the men of the place asked about his wife, he said, "She is my sister," for he was afraid to say, "my wife," thinking, "the men of the place might kill me on account of Rebekah, for she is beautiful."

> It came about, when he had been there a long time, that Abimelech king of the Philistines looked out through a window, and saw, and behold, Isaac was caressing his wife Rebekah.

> Then Abimelech called Isaac and said, "Behold, certainly she is your wife! How then did you say, 'She is my sister'?" And Isaac said to him, "Because I said, 'I might die on account of her.'"

> Abimelech said, "What is this you have done to us? One of the people might easily have lain with your wife, and you would have brought guilt upon us."

> So Abimelech charged all the people, saying, "He who touches this man or his wife shall surely be put to death." Now Isaac sowed in that land and reaped in the same year a hundredfold. And the LORD blessed him. (Genesis 26:6–12)

It's obvious that Isaac didn't trust God to deliver him from Gerar and his countrymen. He felt he had to take matters into his own hands and came up with a deception. But despite Isaac's lack of trust, God delivered him—perhaps because he was the son of Abraham.

More often than we realize, we and our children are delivered from evil because of the righteousness of our fore-fathers.

Now if this was the end of the story, it would be interesting enough, but there remains something very important for us Bible readers. Isaac had only "One Life to Live" and he seems to have lived it almost identically to his father, Abraham. Let's look at the entire twentieth chapter of Genesis:

> Now Abraham journeyed from there toward the land of the Negev, and settled between Kadesh and Shur; then he sojourned in Gerar. Abraham said of Sarah his wife, "She is my sister." So Abimelech king of Gerar sent and took Sarah.

> But God came to Abimelech in a dream of the night, and said to him, "Behold, you are a dead man because of the woman whom you have taken, for she is married." Now Abimelech had not come near her; and he said, "LORD, will You slay a nation, even though blameless? Did he not himself say to me, 'She is my sister'? And she herself said, 'He is my brother.' In the integrity of my heart and the innocence of my hands I have done this."

> Then God said to him in the dream, "Yes, I know that in the integrity of your heart you have done this, and I also kept you from sinning against Me; therefore I did not let you touch her. Now therefore, restore the man's wife, for he is a prophet, and he will pray for you and you will live. But if you do not restore her, know that you shall surely die, you and all who are yours."

> So Abimelech arose early in the morning and called all his servants and told all these things in their hearing; and the men were greatly frightened.

Then Abimelech called Abraham and said to him, "What have you done to us? And how have I sinned against you, that you have brought on me and on my kingdom a great sin? You have done to me things that ought not to be done." And Abimelech said to Abraham, "What have you encountered, that you have done this thing?" Abraham said, "Because I thought, surely there is no fear of God in this place, and they will kill me because of my wife. Besides, she actually is my sister, the daughter of my father, but not the daughter of my mother, and she became my wife; and it came about, when God caused me to wander from my father's house, that I said to her, 'This is the kindness which you will show to me: everywhere we go, say of me, "He is my brother."'"

Abimelech then took sheep and oxen and male and female servants, and gave them to Abraham, and restored his wife Sarah to him. Abimelech said, "Behold, my land is before you; settle wherever you please."

To Sarah he said, "Behold, I have given your brother a thousand pieces of silver; behold, it is your vindication before all who are with you, and before all men you are cleared."

Abraham prayed to God, and God healed Abimelech and his wife and his maids, so that they bore children. For the Lord had closed fast all the wombs of the household of Abimelech because of Sarah, Abraham's wife. (Genesis 20:1–18)

The two stories are so close it's remarkable.

- Abraham sojourned in Gerar, and his son sojourned in Gerar.

- Abimelech was the king in Gerar when Abraham sojourned there. Abimelech, either the same king or a descendant, was the king in Gerar when Isaac sojourned there.

- Evidently there was an inquiry about Abraham's wife as there was about Isaac's wife.

- Abraham lied about Sarah, saying, "She is my sister." Isaac lied about Rebekah, saying, "She is my sister."

- God providentially intervened in both situations and no serious complications occurred.

This is amazing! How could two people, even a father and son, have such similar incidents? How could Isaac's actions so closely resemble those of his father? Why did God choose to record these two incidents in the pages of holy writ?

I'm not sure I have the all the answers to these questions, but I'd like to take a stab at them based upon fifty years of life, forty-two years of Christianity, twenty-eight years of pastoral ministry, and reading through various translations of the Bible about thirty times.

First, the consequences of the sins of the father are visited upon the children to the third and fourth generations. It's possible that Abraham related the story of his experiences with Abimelech to Isaac, and Isaac consciously or subconsciously emulated the actions of his father. But it's also possible that Abraham did not. Either way, we can be reasonably sure that Isaac struggled in some of the same ways as his father:

- He loved beautiful women.
- He had trouble trusting God in difficult situations.

- He would lie if he felt his life was in danger.

We see before us more than just the consequences of Abraham's sins being passed on to Isaac: *We see the very image of his father being passed on to him.* There is a Scripture that I think applies here. "When Adam had lived one hundred and thirty years, he became the father of a son in his own likeness, according to his image, and named him Seth" (Genesis 5:3).

Now that is indeed interesting, since the Bible says something very similar when Adam was created: "Then God said, 'Let Us make man in Our image, according to Our likeness; and let them rule over the fish of the sea and over the birds of the sky and over the cattle and over all the earth, and over every creeping thing that creeps on the earth'" (Genesis 1:26).

- Adam was made in God's image and likeness, but everyone born after Adam is born in Adam's image and likeness.
- Adam was created innocent and sinless, but everyone born after Adam is born in sin and shaped in iniquity.
- Adam was created with God's moral image and likeness, but everyone born after Adam is a fallen image-bearer who is radically corrupted by sin.

Because of Adam's sin, we not only receive the consequences of the sins of our fathers and forefathers all the way back to Adam, we also receive the unique sin nature of our parents and their family lines!

Locked in the infinitely complex genetic code of our parents are the unique qualities, characteristics, idiosyncrasies, and sins of our family lines, and we receive it all from our parents. We have but "One Life to Live." Without the divine intervention of God, Jesus Christ, the Holy Spirit, salvation, and His providence, we will live our lives more like our parents than we ever would imagine! *The probability for reenacting the family mess of our own families is very high.*

Thank God for His divine intervention and providence in the lives of His people. Providence is God's faithful care and effective guidance of everything He has made toward the ends He has chosen. He chose Abraham, called Abraham, sanctified Abraham, and guided Abraham to the positive destiny He had planned for him.

Even in the midst of Abraham's struggle to trust God, his passivity, and his lying, did you notice that God called him a prophet? Did you notice that He blessed the prayers of Abraham to bring about the healing and deliverance of Abimelech's household?

Thank God for His divine intervention and providence, not only in the life of Abraham, but in the life of his son, Isaac. He blessed Isaac and extended to him the promise of his father because of the love and obedience of Abraham. God blessed Isaac and He was not ashamed to be called the God of Abraham and Isaac. That was Isaac's destiny, and that destiny was based upon the grace of God.

The Bible doesn't mention much about Isaac's accomplishments. He was the digger of wells, but his enemies filled up most of his wells. Though we don't see him accomplish a great deal, he was blessed because of his father's love and obedience toward God.

Thank God for His divine intervention and providence in *our* lives. Through the miracle of salvation, Jesus Christ was the Lamb that was slain before the foundation of the world.

- God chose us in Christ before the foundation of the world.

- He chose us and called us that we might bring glory to His name: "These whom He predestined, He also called; and these whom He called, He also justified; and these whom He justified, He also glorified" (Romans 8:30).

- He called us with a holy calling—out of darkness into His marvelous light—to be His children: children of freedom, hope, and destiny.

In short, God has called us to rise above family mess, and He will give us an inheritance among those who are righteous. Since we each have only "One Life to Live," we should leave a godly inheritance to our children, our children's children, and as many as the LORD our God shall call.

Discussion Questions

1. Do you know about any sins that might be family sins?

2. Are any of these family sins impacting you personally? How? If not, what makes you think you escaped
   from their impact?

3. In what ways has God intervened in your life to help
   you rise above the legacy of your family sin and family
   mess?

Chapter Eight

Jacob and Esau
(The Young and the Restless)

We've looked at two generations of Abraham's family: Abraham and Isaac. Remember, because of God's nature, the consequences of the sins of a family will reach the third and fourth generations. So, let's look at Isaac's son, Jacob.

Isaac's wife, Rebekah, was barren. Yet, Isaac prayed for her and she became pregnant. That's interesting. When we can't have children, we go to specialists. But, they prayed. What an idea!

Instead of one baby being conceived there were two, and the babies struggled within Rebekah. This was so disturbing that she asked herself, "If I am pregnant, what is going on inside of me?" So, she inquired of the LORD.

> The LORD said to her, "Two nations are in your womb; and two peoples will be separated from your body; and one people shall be stronger than the other; and the older shall serve the younger." (Genesis 25:23)

This third generation of Abraham's family begins with family mess in the womb. This is a remarkable Scripture! You may ask, "How can two twins struggle even before birth?" The only explanation I can give you lies in the genetics of their mother and father. This was an indication of what was to come.

When it was time for Rebekah to deliver the babies, Esau came out first. They named him Esau, which means *hairy,* because he was covered with red hair. When Esau's brother came out after him, he was holding onto Esau's heal, so they named him Jacob, which means "one who grasps the heel" or "one who supplants or cheats." Family mess marked the gestation of Jacob and Esau and family mess attended their birth. But the worst was yet to come.

As Jacob and Esau grew up, you could readily see the family mess. One of the problems was parental partiality, which fostered continuing hostility between Esau, the opportunistic outdoorsman and hunter, beloved of his father, and Jacob, the quiet, settled, integrated (but sneaky) son, favored by his mother.

The tensions between these brothers seemed to threaten the fulfillment of the divine promise to make a great nation through Abraham, Isaac, and his heir. But which of the twins would be that heir?

Esau was the firstborn, and as such owned the birthright, which was a double portion of the father's assets upon his death. The firstborn's benefits also included a special blessing from the father and the privilege of leadership of the family. The Bible says that Esau despised this birthright (Genesis 25:34), but Jacob coveted it.

It's doubtful that either of the boys understood the long-term importance of the birthright. They certainly didn't understand that it would lead genealogically to the birth of the promised Messiah. Neither did Jacob understand that he coveted something from his earthly father that was already bequeathed to him from his heavenly Father.

> When Jacob had cooked stew, Esau came in from the field and he was famished; and Esau said to Jacob, "Please let me have a swallow of that red stuff there, for I am famished." Therefore his name was called Edom.
>
> But Jacob said, "First sell me your birthright."
>
> Esau said, "Behold, I am about to die; so of what use then is the birthright to me?"
>
> And Jacob said, "First swear to me"; so he swore to him, and sold his birthright to Jacob. Then Jacob gave Esau bread and lentil stew; and he ate and drank, and rose and went on his way. Thus Esau despised his birthright. (Genesis 25:29–34)

Evidently Esau wasn't starving or about to die, or the Bible wouldn't have made that last comment about him despising his birthright. He was just hungry. He thought so little of his birthright and his heritage that he sold it for what amounted to a can of Campbell's vegetable soup.

The first lesson we learn from this particular family mess is this: The birthright of your father is important, but your earthly father can't give you what can only be obtained from your heavenly Father. Therefore, do not ingratiate yourself with your earthly father just to get better stuff in the inheritance, but receive and rest on the birthright that has been promised to you by your heavenly Father.

When you accepted Jesus Christ as your LORD and Savior, you were born into the family of God and adopted into the royal family. Believe it and rest in it. This will allow you to rise above the family mess that may come about when everyone else is caught up in achieving, obtaining, or stealing your earthly father's inheritance.

Which of us has not experienced parental or family partiality in some way? Well, I've got good news for you: *The birthright of heaven is more important than the birthright of earth.* We've received the authority to be sons and daughters of God. From the birthright of earth we receive an earthly inheritance, but from the birthright of heaven we receive a heavenly inheritance.

- We are heirs of the promises of God and joint heirs with Jesus Christ.
- We have received eternal life.
- We have received a destiny that includes an inheritance among those who are righteous.

We don't have to struggle for something that God has already given us. Yet all around me I see people struggling in their families: trying to get something from their mother or father or brothers and sisters, struggling for something that can only come through Jesus Christ.

As we continue to explore the history of Jacob and Esau, it should be clear that we are looking at the history of "The Young and the Restless." We see Esau's youth and restlessness at the end of the twenty-sixth chapter of Genesis. Here the author tells us that Esau married two heathen women and brought grief to his parents. Anyone who has parented a child can understand the grief that Isaac and Rebekah must've felt.

But Jacob was young and restless, too.

Now it came about, when Isaac was old and his eyes were too dim to see, that he called his older son Esau and said to him, "My son." And he said to him, "Here I am."

Isaac said, "Behold now, I am old and I do not know the day of my death. Now then, please take your gear, your quiver and your bow, and go out to the field and hunt game for me; and prepare a savory dish for me such as I love, and bring it to me that I may eat, so that my soul may bless you before I die." (Genesis 27:1–4)

In the Jewish economy, the father bestowed upon the oldest son "The Blessing," which represents God's covenant blessing being passed to the next generation. The blessing included personal, relational, prophetic, and spiritual promises and rewards.

So, Esau went hunting. Now, Rebekah overheard the conversation, and she went to her favorite son, Jacob, and told him what was about to happen. She also told him to follow her plan to steal the blessing.

Rebekah said to her son Jacob, "Behold, I heard your father speak to your brother Esau, saying, 'Bring me some game and prepare a savory dish for me, that I may eat, and bless you in the presence of the LORD before my death.'

"Now therefore, my son, listen to me as I command you. Go now to the flock and bring me two choice young goats from there, that I may prepare them as a savory dish for your father, such as he loves. Then you shall bring it to your father, that he may eat, so that he may bless you before his death." (Genesis 27:6–10)

Rebekah coveted the blessing for her son as much as he coveted it for himself. But, Jacob saw a flaw in her plan. "My brother is a hairy man and I am a smooth man," he said. "If my father feels me, I will get a curse instead of a blessing."

But Rebekah said, "Let the curse be on me. You just do what I tell you to do!"

So Jacob obeyed the voice of his mother instead of relying upon the promise of God. Sound familiar? It's exactly what Isaac did when he obeyed the voice of Rebekah, what Abraham did when he obeyed the voice of Sarah, and what Adam did when he obeyed the voice of Eve.

Dear brother, if you would be a man of God you must cultivate the ability to trust in the Word and promises of God in the face of pressure from important women in your life.

Now, Rebekah made Isaac's favorite dish and put the skin of the young goats on Jacob's hands and on the back of his neck to make him feel like Esau. Then Jacob went in to his father and tricked him out of the blessing. Family mess!

Jacob was a supplanter, a cheater, and a trickster—and his mother was, too. We have seen how the sins or consequences of the father are passed on to the children to the third and fourth generations. But now we see that it works with mothers, too. Jacob was not only being impacted by his father's family mess, but his mother's family mess as well. We'll see in another chapter that Rebekah got her deceptive nature from her own family line.

What a sad situation. Isaac loved Esau, and Jacob obviously coveted that love. Rebekah loved Jacob, and we're not sure what kind of impact that had upon Esau, but it was probably negative. Here's a father and a mother tearing their own family apart, which led to more family mess.

If you, dear brother or sister, have children, then I ask you to consider whether you've shown partiality for one over the other. This is not to hold you responsible for your children's actions; just honestly consider whether or not you may have contributed to any problems by favoring one over the other. If so, please do everything you can to make it right.

Esau sold Jacob the birthright and Jacob tricked Esau out of the blessing—but none of it had to happen. Jacob's birthright and blessing had already been prophesied and fixed. He coveted and wrestled with his earthly father for things that were already promised to him by his heavenly father. He wrestled with his earthly father for that which was already his from his heavenly father.

- Jacob didn't realize who he was—the progenitor of Jesus Christ.
- Jacob didn't realize the magnificent promises that were his.
- Jacob didn't realize his destiny.

It's a sad fact of life that we often struggle to get from our families what we already have in Jesus Christ. "I just wish my mother would show love to me one time." Well, I've got someone better than that who can love you. His name is Jesus. "I just wish that somebody would approve of something I do." I've got someone who can give you eternal approval, and His name is Jesus.

Our heavenly heritage is in Jesus Christ—our identity should be, too. We're priests and kings who've been born and adopted into the family of God. We have magnificent promises in our LORD and Savior, Jesus Christ. Our destiny is to reign with Jesus Christ from the throne of David in the

New Jerusalem. We should rest in that inheritance and stop struggling for an earthly one.

Let's get back to the story. As soon as Jacob left his father, having stolen the blessing, Esau came in from the field with his dish of savory meat. Isaac asked, "Who are you?" and Esau said, "I am your firstborn son, Esau!"

Now we come to the height of family mess. The Bible says that Isaac trembled violently because he realized that he had been tricked. He told his son what had happened, and Esau cried a great and bitter cry and begged for a blessing—but alas, that which he once took for granted was now gone. So Esau swore to kill his brother.

Rebekah called Jacob, told him about his brother's threats, and urged him to go to live with her brother, Laban, until Esau's anger subsided. Her sin separated her from the son she loved and sent him like a vagrant through the land. Though the Bible doesn't say, it appears that Rebekah never saw Jacob again.

Let's survey the family mess:

- *Isaac trembled at the deception.* Isaac was devastated. We don't know what happened with his relationship with Rebekah, because there are no more references to her in the Old Testament except when she is buried, but we can imagine that this incident probably damaged their relationship **significantly**.
- Esau was tormented, angered, embittered, and vengeful.
- Rebekah was, no doubt, greatly grieved by the departure of her beloved son, who—in all probability—she never saw again.

- *Jacob was bereft of his whole family, his home, his homeland, and his peace.* He traveled to the homeland and people of his mother—only to be cheated and tricked himself.

Let me offer some observations to wrap up this portion of our study of the history of Abraham's family. *Observation #1:* It's now clear that the consequences of Abraham's sins were passed on to Isaac and that the consequences of both their sins were passed on to Jacob. Someone should have stopped this deadly chain through repentance.

Praise God that we can stop some of the mess in our families—if we repent. We can't stop all of it, but we can make life significantly different for our children. If we don't repent, our children will carry and finish our pain. Are you willing to say, "The buck stops here—I will be the last link in the chain of this family mess"? I pray you will be that last link.

Observation #2: The rules of dysfunctional families (don't talk, don't feel, don't trust) are evident in the lives of Abraham, his son, and his grandson.

Abraham didn't talk about much; he was very passive. Isaac didn't talk or confront anyone; he was very passive. And now Jacob passively listens to his mother instead of confronting her or at least choosing another course of action. It's also obvious that Abraham and Sarah did not talk to one another. Likewise Isaac and Rebekah did not talk so, it stands to reason that Jacob and his wife would be plagued with the same sickness.

Let's look again at these three rules again.

Don't trust. Throughout these stories, there's an unhealthy trust. Abraham, Isaac, and Jacob didn't trust those they should have trusted, and they trusted those they shouldn't have trusted.

- Abraham didn't trust God.
- Sarah didn't trust Abraham.
- Isaac didn't trust God.
- Rebekah and Jacob didn't trust Isaac.
- Jacob should have trusted God, the prophecies, and his father, but he didn't.
- Jacob shouldn't have trusted his mother.
- Esau didn't trust anybody.

Don't talk. Neither Isaac, Rebekah, Jacob, nor Esau talked about what was going on. Family secrets are a dead giveaway to codependency or family sin. The power of family sin lies in its secrecy. The way to rob family sin of its power is to talk about it with someone who is compassionate and trustworthy. Even if you don't share with another person, talk about it to God in prayer.

Don't feel. Throughout these stories there's an amazing absence of feeling. There's no apparent feeling of remorse or repentance over sin committed against another person. Neither Rebekah nor Jacob seemed to feel the impact or realize the damage of their actions. There is little reporting of people coming face-to-face with their feelings and sharing those feelings with others, or stopping damaging actions, or learning from those actions. The characters think, speak, take actions, and experience personal pain as a result of those actions, but there's very little explanation of their feelings. We can infer that there are strong feelings involved, but they don't seem to be surfaced or confronted.

Our inability to confront our feelings could lead to actions that are sinful, heartless, and cruel.

Observation #3: God's forgiveness is the answer to family sin in each of the passages we've studied. God's forgiveness will prevent a lot of family mess. Before we seek forgiveness, though, we must recognize the sins of our fathers and mothers and how they've uniquely become our sins. When you can face what's going on, and you understand its impact on you, you can ask God for forgiveness. But it's tough to ask God for forgiveness before you've acknowledged that you've done anything wrong.

People today do no wrong. Have you noticed that? They say *if:* "If I've done anything to you, please forgive me" or "If I've sinned . . ." or "If I've hurt you . . ." What's the *if* for? I've just told you that you did hurt me, so where's that *if* coming from?

They won't admit they've done anything wrong; they leave it hanging there like a question. "Well, maybe I did something wrong and maybe I didn't. *If* you can prove that I did it, then I'm sorry." Let's change the *if* to *since.* "Since I hurt you and made a mess of this situation through my sin, I'm asking you to forgive me."

Observation #4: We'll see in the next chapter that God used this family mess to separate Jacob unto Himself. Jacob had to be sent to a far country for some learning experiences. After these experiences, God brings Jacob back home. On his way back home, God wrestled with Jacob, changed his name to Israel, and extended the promises of Abraham and Isaac to him.

Observation #5: We can see God's grace throughout our study of Abraham's family history. God works beneath, behind, through, and beyond family mess to establish His covenant promises to this family. As soon as Jacob left home,

God gave him the dream of the ladder ascending into heaven and reaffirmed His covenant with him—the covenant of Isaac and Abraham.

By the way, did you notice that God didn't reaffirm His covenant with Jacob until after he left home? Sometimes God has to get us away from our families so that He can bring us back home a changed person.

As we become increasingly aware of the family sin and family mess in the line of Abraham, Isaac, and Jacob, it's all the more remarkable to hear God say, "I am the God of Abraham, Isaac, and Jacob." With all of their family mess, He's still pleased to be identified with them and say He's their God.

That brings hope to me. If God worked it out for them, He'll work it out for you and me!

Discussion Questions

1. Are you aware of anything that you have deeply longed for from your father?

2. If you're aware of a deep longing, what have you done to try to get that longing filled by your father? If he is deceased, does that longing now impact you in another way?

3. What do you feel about the fatherhood of God and His ability to fill your deep longing?

4. Are you in competition with a sibling or another person as you pursue your own identity?

5. How has this competition hurt you and how do you think forgiveness can help you?

Chapter Nine

Wrestling Your Way Out of Family Mess
(Guiding Light 2)

In this chapter, we will again see God work beneath, behind, through and beyond family mess to establish His covenant and promises to Jacob. But before we get to our text, we need a little background.

It's interesting to me that it says in Genesis 29:1: "Then Jacob went on his journey, and came to the land of the sons of the east." We have noted that moving towards the east seems to indicate moving towards the world. When Jacob chose to listen to his mother, he chose a path that eventually led him away from the Promised Land and toward the way of the world. When we choose to listen to someone or something other than the Word of God, we choose to leave the Promised Land of abundant Christian living for the way of the world!

After his journey, Jacob settled with Laban, Rebekah's brother, and worked for him for many years. As we take a brief look at the relationship between Laban and Jacob, we see that Rebekah was very much like her brother. Their own family's mess had deeply impacted both of them.

Laban tricked Jacob repeatedly during his stay. The biggest trick involved Laban's daughter, Rachel, whom Jacob loved.

Jacob arranged with Laban to pay Rachel's dowry price by giving him seven years of labor. But at the end of that time, Laban tricked Jacob and sent Rachel's older sister, Leah, into the wedding tent instead. Jacob didn't realize the switch until morning.

I know that sounds confusing. How could this man have sex with somebody and not know who it was? For one thing, it was dark. There were no electric lights. All they had were candles and oil lamps. For another thing, women in that day (unlike women of today) were covered up in every possible way, including veils over their faces. They were covered all through the wedding and covered still at night.

Because it was dark, Leah was covered, and this occurred after a night of festivities with lots of drinking, Jacob didn't recognize her until the morning light appeared. But, as the morning light crept into their tent, there was Leah, in the place of the woman he expected to find. It may be funny to us, but it wasn't funny to him.

When Jacob confronted Laban, he was told about the custom of the older daughter marrying before the younger daughter. Laban said he could have Rachel if he agreed to seven *more* years of labor. Jacob was trapped because he loved Rachel, so he worked fourteen years for her. This is also a touching love story, isn't it?

Jacob worked twenty years for Laban: fourteen years to earn Laban's two daughters and six years to earn his own flock. During his employment, Laban changed Jacob's wages ten times. Now we see where Rebekah's family mess comes from.

This was the outcome of Jacob tricking his father and brothers for things that only God could give him. When we follow this path, we experience a similar outcome. We end up losing the promised land of abundant Christian living *and* we end up living down in the world with sinners who will trick us on every hand.

But, Jacob makes a statement that puts the exclamation point on all that had happened: "Yet your father has cheated me and changed my wages ten times; however, God did not allow him to hurt me" (Genesis 31:7). Jacob could see that God had overruled ten wage changes and twenty years of family mess!

Here's a powerful truth we all need to realize: When God is for you and has a destiny for you, He will not allow family mess to ultimately hurt you. No weapon formed against you can prosper!

In spite of all that Jacob had done, God did not abandon him. Once again, he received God's "guiding light." "Then the LORD said to Jacob, 'Return to the land of your fathers and to your relatives, and I will be with you'" (Genesis 31:3).

Sometimes God separates us from our relatives because His high calling for us demands total separation. He did this with Abraham. But sometimes God separates us from our relatives, because His high calling prepares us to return and minister to our relatives.

Did you get that? Many people may be secretly delighted to be away from relatives they don't like or who bring family mess into their lives. Well, God didn't separate you from them because of your likes and dislikes. He didn't separate you because of your will, but because of His will. He may want you to go back to them.

That's what He wanted from Jacob. So Jacob gathered up his wives, his children, and all the livestock that the LORD had blessed him with, and he journeyed back to Canaan, the Promised Land—the land of his destiny.

But even as Jacob left Laban's home, more family mess happened. Jacob left without telling Laban, and as they departed, Rachel stole the household idols. This confirms what we learned earlier: i.e. that Abraham's father and family were idol worshipers.

You're probably thinking, "But that's Rebekah's family line, not Abraham's!" Well, Laban's father was Bethuel, and Bethuel's father was Nahor, and Nahor was *Abraham's brother.* So Laban is the grandson of Abraham's brother. Chances are, Abraham would've had household gods, too, had it not been for the grace of God!

Imagine what you might have left over from your own family mess were it not for the grace of God! The next time you look at your family and say, "I don't know what's wrong with those people," remember that but for the grace of God you would be just like them. God delivered you and lifted you out from among them, because there's something He wants to do with you. But without God, you could be just like those people. So praise God and don't judge them.

When Laban discovered that Jacob was gone and his household gods were missing, he pursued Jacob to recover them. When he overtook Jacob he asked him why he deceived him by leaving secretly and not giving him the opportunity to kiss his sons and daughters and send them away with joy. He also accused Jacob of stealing his gods.

You can tell by Laban's language that he wasn't concerned with kissing his relatives or sending them away with joy, because he still referred to them as *his.*

Here's something to think about: It's sad when you have a god that someone can steal! If you worship anything that can be taken away—like a house, car, a piece of furniture, money, health, good looks, or another person—you're asking for trouble and your house is built on sinking sand.

Jacob told Laban the truth; he was afraid that Laban would take his daughters from him by force. Jacob told him to search their belongings, and whoever was found with the gods would die. He didn't know that Rachel had stolen the gods.

Laban couldn't find the idols, because Rachel sat on them and used the excuse of being on her period for not getting up. Family mess! Rachel had learned deception well from her father.

So Jacob journeyed on. As he neared his home, he sent messengers to Esau to see if he was still angry, and he set up camp and prayed. His prayer is worth repeating.

O God of my father Abraham and God of my father Isaac, O LORD, who said to me, "Return to your country and to your relatives, and I will prosper you," I am unworthy of all the lovingkindness and of all the faithfulness which You have shown to Your servant; for with my staff only I crossed this Jordan, and now I have become two companies.

Deliver me, I pray, from the hand of my brother, from the hand of Esau; for I fear him, that he will come and attack me and the mothers with the children. For You said, "I will surely prosper you and make your descendants as the sand of the sea, which is too great to be numbered." (Genesis 32:9–12)

Let's examine a few things about this prayer:

- Jacob addressed God as the God of Abraham and Isaac, and as Yahweh (or Jehovah).
- He acknowledged his unworthiness.
- He acknowledged God's physical blessings.
- He asked for protection from Esau. (Notice that the "give me" part didn't start until way down in the prayer. We *start* with, "LORD, give me . . . I need . . . You know that Your child needs . . ." But there are some things we should address before we get down there!)
- He reminded God of His covenant promise.

Then Jacob divided his family into two groups. He thought, "If Esau is still angry and attacks, one of the two groups will be able to escape."

All of that is background for the text I want to deal with in this chapter. It's in Genesis 32.

> Now he arose that same night and took his two wives and his two maids and his eleven children, and crossed the ford of the Jabbok. He took them and sent them across the stream. And he sent across whatever he had. Then Jacob was left alone, and a man wrestled with him until daybreak. When he saw that he had not prevailed against him, he touched the socket of his thigh; so the socket of Jacob's thigh was dislocated while he wrestled with him.
>
> Then he said, "Let me go, for the dawn is breaking." But he said, "I will not let you go unless you bless me." So he said to him, "What is your name?" And he said, "Jacob." He said, "Your name shall no longer be Jacob,

but Israel; for you have striven with God and with men and have prevailed."

Then Jacob asked him and said, "Please tell me your name." But he said, "Why is it that you ask my name?" And he blessed him there.

So Jacob named the place Peniel, for he said, "I have seen God face to face, yet my life has been preserved." Now the sun rose upon him just as he crossed over Penuel, and he was limping on his thigh. Therefore, to this day the sons of Israel do not eat the sinew of the hip which is on the socket of the thigh, because he touched the socket of Jacob's thigh in the sinew of the hip. (Genesis 32:22–32)

Let me point out some things from this story as they relate to family mess.

Point #1: God wrestled with Jacob to deliver him from family mess. Jacob didn't challenge God to a wrestling match, God engaged Jacob. If it was Jacob wrestling with someone, he might have tried to gain something from that man. But here it appears that the man was trying to gain something from Jacob. I believe God wanted Jacob to see what a poor, feeble, worthless creature he was. *God wanted to bring Jacob to the end of himself.*

God has a purpose in wrestling with us. He wants to bring us to the dawning of a new day, but He can only do that by bringing us to the end of ourselves. Sometimes He puts us in a submission hold—He's not asking us to say *uncle,* but *Jesus!* But we struggle for a blessing; we struggle to hold onto ourselves. Instead we must learn to give in and say, "Jesus! You are the LORD and Master of my life."

Family mess can bring you to the end of yourself. It can bring you to the point where you say, "There's nothing I can do with my mother!" Family mess can bring you to the point where you recognize there is nothing you can do with your children, or your aunt and uncle, or spouse. There's nothing I can do with these people! They're in God's hands! They're there anyway, but sometimes He has to use family mess to make us realize it and let go.

"In countless scenarios, each one of us will stay the way we are until something forces us to change—perhaps a crisis, God, or both. We won't make the hard choices until we have to" (Psalm 119:67). In Jacob's case, it was both. God brought Jacob to the point of realizing there was nothing he could do about his situation. His mother had messed him up, his father let it happen, his brother was out to murder him—and there was nothing he could do about any of it.

God often uses crises of family mess to change us and call us to our higher walk. He'll call us out of that family mess; He'll call us out of that divorce; He'll call us out of those relatives who don't like us; He'll call us out of those things to make us come on up a little bit higher. Let family mess do its work.

Point #2: God wrestled with Jacob until daybreak. "The reference to dawn indicates that his struggle continued for a good while." God is a patient Wrestler. He doesn't mind wrestling with us until He can effect the dawning of a new day in our lives. This match is not the best two out of three falls, and there are no time limits. He wants to bring us out of the night of death to a morning of resurrection. God wants to raise us to new life out of the death of family mess!

Do you want to be delivered from family mess? If you don't, there's no use in my talking about it. Do you think that's a strange question? Doesn't everybody want to be delivered! No, they don't.

That's why Jesus asked the man at the pool at Siloam, "Do you wish to be here?" When the water is troubled you sit there and say, "I don't have anybody to put me in." Is it about someone putting you in or is it about getting into the water? If it's the latter, when you think the pool is about to be troubled, start crawling and doing anything you can to get into that water to obtain healing. If you want to be healed, don't sit there and complain that there's no one to put you in the water. Ask yourself the same question Jesus asked: "Do I want to be made whole?"

Some of us want to end our wrestling match with God by avoiding our families, in an attempt to avoid family mess. But God allows and uses family mess because He's wrestling to bring about the dawning of a new day in our lives. We don't have to live in the death of family mess when we have the living promise of Jehovah God.

Point #3: God wrestled with Jacob until the socket of his thigh was dislocated. "When Jacob wrestled against God's divine dealing with him, 'God touched the hollow of his thigh; and the hollow of Jacob's thigh was out of joint as He wrestled with him.' The sentence of death had to be written on the flesh."

- God wrestled with Jacob until his flesh was crucified.
- God wrestled with Jacob until the genetic source of his family mess was broken.
- God wrestled with Jacob until He lifted him above the influence of his gene pool.
- Jacob had to have his flesh broken.
- He had to have his family sin broken.

Likewise, for Jesus to deliver us from our family mess:

- We must have our flesh crucified.
- We must have our dependence upon our genetic heritage broken.
- We must be raised above the influence of our gene pools, which is often seen in the patterns of our fathers.
- We must experience brokenness.
- We must have our family sin broken.

There comes a point in Christianity when God will kick everything away from you—your friends, your staffs, your crutches—everything that you ever depended upon, everything you thought would hold you up. God will kick it out from under you because you must come to depend solely upon Him. Praise God for the end result, but the process is painful.

"Jacob carried the marks of this encounter with him all his life, in the dislocation of his thigh . . . By the dislocation of his thigh the carnal nature of his previous wrestling was declared to be powerless and wrong" (Genesis 32:24–32). For the rest of his days, Jacob had a built-in reminder that the flesh can never accomplish what only the Spirit can bring to pass.

We need the power of our flesh dislocated. We need the power of our carnal natures dislocated. We need the brokenness of our flesh as a reminder that we can never wrestle from relatives or accomplish with our own power that which only the Spirit can bring to pass!

Many Christians haven't discovered this yet. They're still trying to walk under their own power, walk in their own accord, straighten out their own messes, and work through their own trouble. Maybe that's you, too. You don't recognize that you're crippled and can't do it. You need to be picked up by the power of the Holy Spirit and carried in the arms of Jesus Christ. You need to let Him work things out for you, in your family, where you thought things could never be worked out. Jesus can move into your family situation and do some powerful things.

Point #4: God wrestled with Jacob to change his name. In ancient Jewish culture one's name represented one's character. The name Jacob received from his family meant one who grasps the heel of another, supplanter, cheater. But God gave him a new name representing who he was in the family of God. His new name, Israel, means "he fights or persists with God."

Although it was God who engaged him, Jacob wrestled with God and man and he prevailed. He prevailed with God in prayer. Hosea reinforces this:

> In the womb he took his brother by the heel, and in his maturity he contended with God. Yes, he wrestled with the angel and prevailed; he wept and sought His favor. (Hosea 12:3–4a)

The phrase *sought His favor* is the Hebrew word *chanan*, which means "to pray or make supplication."[1] One of the major ways to overcome family mess is to wrestle it into submission through the spiritual discipline of prayer. Prevail upon God in prayer to deliver you from family mess.

When you prevail upon God in prayer and He crucifies your reliance upon your flesh and your family, God gives you a new name, which represents who you are in Him.

- You're no longer called a sinner, but a saint.
- You're no longer called a slave, but a friend.
- You're no longer called an acquaintance, but a brother or sister.
- You're no longer called a laborer, but a priest and king or queen.
- You're no longer called a guest of the wedding, but the Bride of Christ.

Point #5: God wrestled with Jacob until He blessed him.

- He blessed Jacob with the covenant promises of Abraham and Isaac.
- He blessed Jacob with a new name, which represented a major change in Jacob's life.
- He blessed Jacob to return to the land of his birth, the Promised Land.
- And there were more blessings to come.

But God couldn't or wouldn't give Jacob the blessings He still had in store, until He and Jacob wrestled the family mess into submission.

God *used* family mess in Jacob's life.

- He sent him away from home that He might bring him back.
- He left home running for his life; he returned with the promise of his life.
- He left home to follow the course of the world; he returned by the prophecy of God.

- He left the Promised Land not understanding what he had; he returned with God's assurance that the land was his.
- He left home empty; he came back full.
- He left home with no fellowship with God; he came back having experienced the intimacy of wrestling with God.
- He left home with a name that meant "cheater"; he came back with one that meant "one who has prevailed with God."
- He left home confused; he came back certain of his destiny.
- He left home immature, frightened, and passive; he came back experienced, confident, and assertive.
- He left home because of family mess; he returned having conquered it.

God will engage us in a big-time wrestling match until He crushes the flesh of our family mess and we wrestle our family mess into submission!

Discussion Questions

1. Describe your big-time wrestling match with God.

2. Who's winning?

3. In what ways has God crippled you and what does that mean to you?

4. In what ways has God changed your name and what does that mean to you?

5. What family member is God preparing you to minister to?

---

1. *NASB Greek and Hebrew Dictionary,* New American Standard, Copyright © 1960, 1963, 1968, 1971, 1972, 1975, 1977, 1988, by the Lockman Foundation. All rights reserved. Database c. NavPress Software.

Chapter Ten

Roots
(All in the Family)

Jacob inherited a double measure of family mess. It came from both sides of his family. Allow me to trace the confluence of these two streams of family mess that joined to negatively impact Jacob's life. Let's look at the "Roots" of family mess in the life of Jacob, "The Young and the Restless."

First, from his father's side of the family:

- Jacob's great-grandfather, Terah, was an idol worshiper.
- His grandfather, Abraham, was a passive man who had trouble trusting God.
- His father, Isaac, was a passive man who had trouble trusting God.
- Jacob, himself, was a passive man who had trouble trusting God.
- Abraham worshipped idols, but was delivered by the grace of God.

Here's the family mess Jacob inherited from his mother's side:

- Jacob's grandfather, Nahor, was an idol worshiper. (This is Rebekah's father, Abraham's brother, and is not to be confused with Abraham's grandfather, who was also named Nahor.)
- Since Rebekah's grandfather, father, and brother were all idol worshipers, it's likely that Rebekah worshiped idols, too.
- Jacob's wives, Rachel and Leah (who were Laban's daughters and thus from his mother Rebekah's side of the family), worshiped idols.
- As we'll see in this chapter, idol worship manifested itself as a stronghold sin in Jacob's household.
- Jacob's mother, Rebekah, and her brother, Laban, were tricksters, which leads us to believe that their father, Nahor, may have been a trickster.
- Jacob's wife, Rachel, Laban's daughter, was a trickster who coveted and stole her father's household gods.

The joint influence of both sides of the family impacted Jacob greatly. Naturally and genetically, Jacob was inclined to be a passive trickster who would have trouble trusting God and would gravitate towards idol worship.

You should become aware of the mighty river of family mess that has converged in you from the two streams of your family. Take a deep look at your "Roots" to see what you've inherited.

If we can step back from feeling the impact of the river of family mess and closely examine our roots, I think we'll come to the conclusion that many of things that we're facing are "All in the Family!"

- Alcoholism—"All in the Family."
- Anger—"All in the Family."
- Chronic depression—"All in the Family."
- Negativity—"All in the Family."
- Passivity—"All in the Family."
- Relationship addictions—"All in the Family."
- Physical abuse—"All in the Family."
- Sexual abuse—"All in the Family."
- Sexual idolatry—"All in the Family."
- Substance abuse—"All in the Family."

One of the most curious things about many Christians is their ability to see some of the deep mess of their family and yet believe that it did not impact them. "Oh, yes, there is some deep family mess in my family. I'm so glad it skipped my generation." I've got news for you: It *didn't* skip your generation. You might be able to rise above family mess by the grace of God, but you're a part of the stream of your family mess. Don't be deceived: The family mess you've inherited will impact you in some way.

In spite of the great family mess that flowed to and through Jacob, there was still great hope for him. That hope lay in the words of Jehovah: "I am the God of Abraham, Isaac, *and Jacob.*"

Jehovah God worked through all of this genetic and environmental family mess to give Jacob the covenant promises and destiny that He had ordained for Him. Jacob's roots did not stop God from blessing him. The family mess, which Jacob inherited, did not stop God from bringing about his destiny.

If God did this for Jacob, He will do it for you. Your roots need not disqualify you from the blessings of Jehovah God. This is great news! When you accept Christ as your personal Savior, you are engrafted into Him. You become a part of a new tree with a new root system.

- Jesus is the root of Jesse who grew up out of dry ground.
- Jesus is the green tree of Jehovah God.
- Jesus is the tree of life whose leaves are good for the healing of the nation.
- Jesus is the tree that is planted by the rivers of water, whose leaves and fruit do not wither.
- Jesus is the vine and we are the branches, and we receive the flow of life, joy, and blessings from Him.

We've now followed the iniquity of Abraham down through the third generation, to Jacob. But our key verse says that God visits the iniquity of the fathers on the children to the third *and fourth* generations. We're finally ready to move on to the fourth generation to see how the consequences of Abraham's sins play themselves out.

Let's jump back to the time before Jacob left Laban's home to return to the Promised Land. Rachel, his best-loved wife, could not have children. As we've seen, in Bible times that was the worst possible plight of a woman. Yet God opened the womb of Leah, the less-loved wife. That seems like poetic justice to me: The one who is less honored by Humanity often receives the greater blessing from God.

When Rachel saw that she couldn't have children, she gave Jacob her handmaid, Bilhah, as a surrogate mother. But in due time God blessed Rachel to have children. Not surprisingly, her two sons became the ones best loved by Jacob.

In the meantime, Leah had stopped having children. So she did what Rachel had done: She gave Jacob her handmaid, Zilpah, as a surrogate mother. Jacob had two wives, two surrogate mothers, twelve sons, and one daughter. Family mess and "All My Children!"

We've already seen this handmaid scenario in the life of Abraham and Sarah, but here it's doubled. *That which is tolerated by one generation is accepted by the next, and that which is accepted by one generation is embraced by the next.* When we don't stop the family mess, when we don't stop the lying, the addictions or the anger, it only gets worse. Each generation gets a little farther away from God.

So, what kind of impact do you think this whole situation had upon Jacob's children? I believe they were certainly aware of this whole mess, and it must have had a negative impact upon them.

But even if this didn't negatively impact the children, there was another scenario that almost certainly involved them in family mess. This story involves Reuben, Leah's firstborn.

> Now in the days of wheat harvest Reuben went and found mandrakes in the field, and brought them to his mother Leah. Then Rachel said to Leah, "Please give me some of your son's mandrakes."
>
> But she said to her, "Is it a small matter for you to take my husband? And would you take my son's mandrakes

also?" So Rachel said, "Therefore he may lie with you tonight in return for your son's mandrakes."

When Jacob came in from the field in the evening, then Leah went out to meet him and said, "You must come in to me, for I have surely hired you with my son's mandrakes." So he lay with her that night. (Genesis 30:14–16)

What a mess! Two women bargaining for the sexual favors of their husband, using their children's goods as bargaining chips. A mandrake was a small, perennial plant native to the Middle East. Although not grown for food, its root and berries are edible. The Ancient Near East viewed it as an aphrodisiac and fertility drug. An aphrodisiac is something that arouses or increases sexual desire. It's often called a love apple or devil's apple.

Since these women were basically vying to have the most children, the mandrakes would be seen as a competitive edge. No wonder Rachel wanted them. And no wonder Leah used them to advance her chances of fertility. In such a situation, we have to imagine that the children would be caught in the middle. Family mess.

Rachel and Leah were probably using the children to communicate to one another. I can see them sending their children back and forth with messages and mandrakes. This is called *triangulation,* and it is a symptom of dysfunctionality. Triangulation is learned in childhood: It gives the child a sense of power to be included and involved in the lives of others. But sometimes that involvement can backfire and both parties can get angry with the child. Triangulation can become emotionally exhausting and frustrating.

What does triangulation look like? Parents using children to carry messages like: "Tell your mother I'm angry with her," "Tell your father I'm not going out tonight," "Tell your mother to go to the doctor," and "Tell your father to get a new suit."

Did your parents do this to you? If so, recognize it. And don't do it your children!

If only this were all the mess in Jacob's family, but it isn't. In the thirty-fourth chapter of Genesis, we come to a very sordid story. The passage is too long to include, so let me relate it to you.

The incident takes place in Shechem, a city in Canaan, and with the sons of Hamor. Shechem, the son of Hamor the Hivite, raped Dinah, the daughter of Jacob and Leah. After the rape, Shechem was still deeply attracted to Dinah and loved her. So, he asked his father to get Dinah for him to be his wife. When Dinah's brothers heard what had happened they were very angry.

Hamor spoke first to Jacob about arranging a marriage, and then he talked to Dinah's brothers. Hamor proposed a treaty that would join their two peoples as one. But because Dinah's brothers were angry, they lied to Hamor. They said, "We will accept the conditions of your treaty, if you and all your people will agree to be circumcised. If you won't agree to be circumcised, we cannot possibly accept the terms of your agreement."

The request seemed reasonable to Hamor and Shechem, so Shechem did not delay in meeting the terms of the agreement, because he delighted in Dinah.

Since Shechem was more respected than all of his father's household, he and his father went to the city gates and presented the proposal to the men of the city. They told them,

"We can prosper in a number of ways if we unite with this people: We can intermarry with them and trade with them, and they have much livestock. But there is one condition: We must be circumcised!" Believe it or not, all of the men of the city agreed and were circumcised.

Now comes the sneaky part. On the third day after their circumcision, when all the men of the city were incapacitated from pain, Simeon and Levi (two of Dinah's brothers) sneaked up on the city and killed every man with swords.

The sin we saw in Abraham was bad enough, but it wasn't as bad as what we saw in Isaac. But what we saw in Isaac wasn't as bad as what we saw in Jacob—which isn't as bad as what we see when we get to his sons; to the third and fourth generations!

Now the family mess in Jacob's line included murder—even genocide! I wish that were all, but there's more. To sibling rivalry and murder, we can add idol worship.

Let's jump forward in the story to after Jacob returned to the Promised Land and met his brother Esau.

We know that Rachel stole her father's household gods. But now we see that she didn't steal them just to have them—she stole them to worship them. It appears that idol worship continued in the household of Jacob for years, and it seems that Jacob allowed it. That's not unusual, considering that his father and grandfather were very passive towards their wives.

> Then God said to Jacob, "Arise, go up to Bethel and live there, and make an altar there to God, who appeared to you when you fled from your brother Esau."

> So Jacob said to his household and to all who were with him, "Put away the foreign gods which are among you, and purify yourselves and change your garments; and

let us arise and go up to Bethel, and I will make an altar there to God, who answered me in the day of my distress and has been with me wherever I have gone."

So they gave to Jacob all the foreign gods which they had and the rings which were in their ears, and Jacob hid them under the oak which was near Shechem. (Genesis 35:1–4)

The earrings may have been magical with words engraved on them that were to supposedly ward off evil. Family mess. Check your family to see if they have any amulets or trinkets or jewelry that may have something demonic attached to them. If so, don't wear them!

These children of Jacob were a long way from worshiping God. Unfortunately, sibling rivalry, murder, and idol worship were not the only elements in Jacob's family mess.

In the midst of all this family mess, we also get stories implying that sexual idolatry or addiction was a problem. I use the term sexual idolatry because whenever anyone is addicted to some form of sexuality, it becomes an idol.

We see Reuben again, this time revealing that he had a problem with sexual idolatry: "It came about while Israel was dwelling in that land, that Reuben went and lay with Bilhah his father's concubine, and Israel heard of it" (Genesis 35:22a). Now we can add incest to the list of sordid mess in Jacob's family. By the way, Jacob—whom God had since renamed "Israel"—didn't confront Reuben about this. He reacted just like his father and grandfather would have: with passivity.

What about you? Are there situations in your family in which sexual sin was committed, but no one has dealt with it?

I'm sorry to say it, but there's more. Two other incidents of sexual idolatry involved Judah, another one of Leah's sons. First he had sex with a Canaanite woman, who produced two children. The Bible doesn't say that they were married, so I assume that Judah participated in illicit, premarital sex. In the second incident, Judah used the services of what he thought was a prostitute, but who turned out to be his daughter-in-law in disguise. What a mess! Sexual idolatry, misconduct, and addiction seemed to be a stronghold in Jacob's family.

Do you see how the sins of the fathers are coming to a head in the fourth generation of the children? What a legacy of mess! But don't miss this point, either: Despite it all, the twelve sons of Jacob would become the twelve tribes of the Children of Israel, the people of God, the apple of God's eye. They were God's people whom He chose by grace and blessed because of His gracious promise.

> For you are a holy people to the LORD your God; the LORD your God has chosen you to be a people for His own possession out of all the peoples who are on the face of the earth. The LORD did not set His love on you nor choose you because you were more in number than any of the peoples, for you were the fewest of all peoples, but because the LORD loved you and kept the oath which He swore to your forefathers. (Deuteronomy 7:6–8a)

Regardless of the family mess in your family, if you have accepted Jesus Christ as your personal Savior, you are part of the Church, the body of Jesus Christ, the Bride of the heavenly Bridegroom, the family of God, the sons and daughters of God, who are in Christ Jesus.

That should give you joy! That should give you hope. The world says, "You are nothing but an illegitimate child."

But God says, "You are My Child! I died for you. I have a destiny for you, and I'm taking you where you can spend eternity with Me."

You also have a powerful Scripture that affirms this truth:

Blessed be the God and Father of our LORD Jesus Christ, who has blessed us with every spiritual blessing in the heavenly places in Christ, just as *He chose us in Him before the foundation of the world,* that we would be holy and blameless before Him. *In love He predestined us to adoption as sons* through Jesus Christ to Himself, according to the kind intention of His will, to the praise of the glory of His grace, which He freely bestowed on us in the Beloved. *In Him we have redemption through His blood, the forgiveness of our trespasses, according to the riches of His grace which He lavished on us.* (Ephesians 1:3–8a, emphasis mine)

Throughout eternity He will show you His grace, if you have believed in Him as your personal Savior. He will continually pour out His grace. He will continually lavish it upon you. You see, hope is not in the present, but it is in Jesus. Hope is in the fact that one day God shall right every wrong, straighten everything out, and give you an inheritance. Hope is in the fact that maybe you're not who you think you should be now, but one day—in Jesus—you will be everything He wants you to be and you will walk with Him and He will walk and talk with you. You will spend eternity with God because of what He has done for you, in Christ!

God's grace saved me. His grace lifted me up. His grace He turned me around. His grace He planted my feet on a rock. His grace called me to the ministry. In His grace He gave me a destiny. Because of His grace, my name is written in the Lamb's Book of Life, I'll spend eternity with Him, get a reward, and receive a new name. And He's doing the same thing for you!

If that doesn't excite you, you may never get excited. If that doesn't generate joy in your soul, you may never get any. This should make you happy. Your job can't change your destiny. Your family can't change your destiny. Hard times can't change your destiny. Family mess can't change your destiny. None of these things can change what God has for you in heaven one day. Eyes have not seen and ears have not heard the blessing that God has prepared for those who love Him.

Discussion Questions

1. When you look at the mighty rivers of your mother and father's side of your family, can you see how their family mess flows together to you?

2. Are you aware of any sins or weaknesses in you that have roots in your family history?

3. Have you or are you seeing any triangulation in your family? How has that impacted you?

4. Do you see any evidences of idolatry in your family tree?

5. How do the promises of God, which come along with salvation, help you to face the mess of your family?

Chapter Eleven

Roots 2
(All My Children)

Now that we've surveyed four generations of Abraham's family, we can see how the consequences of his sin facilitated family mess for his family all the way down to his great-grandchildren.

In light of what we've seen, let me expand upon the concepts of dysfunctionality and codependency.

The term *codependent* originally applied only to the spouse, lover, or significant other of someone who was chemically dependent. It's now taken on a life and identity of its own. Many professionals now use codependency as a diagnostic term that refers to a specific set of emotional and behavioral symptoms.

One source explains like this:

> In its broadest sense, *codependency* can be defined as *an addiction to people, behaviors, or things*. Co-dependency is the fallacy of trying to control interior feelings by controlling people, things, and events on the outside. To the codependent, control or lack of it is central to every aspect of life.[1]

Authors John and Linda Friel give a formal definition for codependency in their book *Adult Children: The Secrets of Dysfunctional Families:*

> Co-dependency is a dysfunctional pattern of living which emerges from our family of origin as well as our culture, producing arrested identity development, and resulting in an over-reaction to things outside of us and an under-reaction to things inside of us. Left untreated, it can deteriorate into an addiction.[2]

Psychologists have identified several symptoms connected with codependency, including:

- depression
- tolerance of inappropriate behavior
- dulled or inappropriate emotions
- self-defeating coping strategies
- strong need to control self and others
- stress-related physical symptoms
- abuse of self
- neglect of self
- difficulty with intimacy and/or sexuality
- fear of abandonment
- shame
- inappropriate guilt
- eventual addictions
- rages[3]

These are personal characteristics, but there are also codependent characteristics that apply to families. The dysfunctional characteristics of a family should be looked at as a line with varying degrees of seriousness.

On a continuum from extremely healthy to extremely unhealthy families, you will find some or all of the following characteristics, depending on how functional or dysfunctional a family maybe:

- physical, emotional, or sexual abuse/neglect and vicarious abuse
- perfectionism
- rigid rules, lifestyle, and/or belief systems
- the "no talk rule"—keeping "the family secrets"
- inability to identify and/or express feelings
- triangulation (a communication pattern using one person as intermediary)
- double messages/double binds
- inability to play, have fun, and be spontaneous
- high tolerance for inappropriate behavior/ pain
- enmeshment (the inability to realize where you end and someone else begins).[4]

Some dysfunctional families have few of these characteristics. Some families have all of them.

In Abraham's family, we've covered many sordid stories. But there's one that perfectly sums up the family mess in the fourth generation after him: the story of Joseph.

You'd think that Jacob would have learned something from the conditions he grew up in. He'd seen the impact of parental favoritism. Perhaps he'd even said to himself, "When I have a family, I'll never do what my parents did!" But here is Jacob doing exactly what was done to him. The Bible tells us that Jacob loved Joseph more than all his other sons, and it showed. He was asking for family mess.

When Joseph was seventeen years old, he was pasturing Jacob's flock with his brothers. Evidently Joseph would keep an eye on his brothers while they were shepherding Jacob's herds, and then report back to his father. So, he came home one day and squealed on his brothers.

The situation was complicated by the fact that Jacob loved Joseph more than all of his sons, because he was the son of his old age—and the first by Rachel, his favorite wife. Jacob made it worse by showing his preference for Joseph by making him a multicolored tunic. The Bible tells us that the other brothers hated Joseph for being their father's favorite. They couldn't even speak to him on friendly terms. Family mess!

Just as Jacob's father had preferred Esau to him, and his mother had preferred him to Esau, now Jacob preferred Joseph to his other sons. Jacob was passing the family mess of his father to his own sons. His unfinished business with his father would be picked up and finished by his sons. Jacob's pain is carried by and manifested in his sons. Some of the tragic things that they do may simply be a way of seeking attention and affection from their father. When people don't get the love they need, they may settle for any attention, positive or negative.

Serious sibling rivalry is a blight on any family. It's ugly to see one child spoiled by favoritism and another child rejected. Both children will carry the pain of their father deep into adulthood. The spoiled child is actually set up for some form of failure, because life will not treat that child the same way as the father did. On the other hand, the rejected child will likely search for love and acceptance for the rest of his or her life.

Here's a word of advice for parents with more than one child: each child is different and must be related to differently and loved differently. I believe it is impossible to love two children equally, because each child is a unique gift of God, but you must do all that you can to keep from showing favoritism for one child over another.

Although you can't love each child exactly the same or in exactly the same way, you *can* love each child *to the same extent*. You can go to the same lengths for each child. I am not sure how well I did with my children, but I tried to go to the same lengths for each of them.

- I tried to go to both of their events, although their events were different.

- I tried to spend money on things that were important to them, although those things were drastically different.

- I tried to spend time with each of them; doing what each wanted to do.

Are you getting the picture? Are you doing this with your children? Did your parents do this with you? If they didn't, if they showed preference, you're probably inclined to show preference among your children. And you're probably still hurting. If this is you, examine your background. It's worth the pain to examine and wrestle your way out of family mess, so you can stop this pain from being passed on to your children.

Now, back to Joseph. About this time, Joseph had a dream. The dream was about his destiny and was in keeping with the destiny that flowed through Abraham, Isaac, and Jacob. The dream seemed to prophesy Joseph's rise to a place of authority and prominence in the world, which included the bowing down of his brothers before him.

Joseph didn't keep the dream to himself; he told his brothers. Family mess! Although there is little negative information about Joseph in the Bible, he didn't escape the family mess. The impact of family mess on Joseph is evident: He seemed to flaunt his father's favoritism in his brothers' faces.

- *He wore that coat of many colors with pride.* He seemed oblivious to the impact of his actions upon his brothers. Instead of holding it until Friday night at the bar mitzvah, he immediately came out wearing that leather coat with all those colors. He sashayed in front of his brothers. If you have siblings, you know what he probably said: "I've got something you don't have!"
- *He tattled on them.*
- *He told them the dream with no regard to their feelings.* It doesn't seem that the dream was for them: It was for him. The dream was God telling him, "I'm going to do something for you." But Joseph had to go and tell everybody else.

No, Joseph didn't escape the family mess in his family. But by the grace of God he did rise above it!

This story shows us not only Joseph's family mess but that of his brothers, too. When his brothers heard the dream, they hated him even more. They hated their own brother. How many of us hate our own relatives? Maybe you'd better not answer that.

Then Joseph had another dream. This time the dream indicated that in addition to his brothers, his father and mother would one day bow down before him. He also shared this dream with his brothers, and they hated him even more. More family mess!

Finally, Joseph decided to tell his parents about this dream. This brought his father's rebuke, in addition to more hatred from his brothers. The prophecy, which told of God's destiny for Joseph, didn't bring encouragement, happiness, or affirmation—at first. The dream brought him loneliness, misunderstanding, hatred, mistreatment, rebuke, and jealousy from his family members.

Satan uses family mess, loneliness, misunderstanding, hatred, mistreatment, rebuke, and jealousy to discourage God's prophecy, promise, and destiny in our lives. He would have us think: "If my own mother doesn't like me, then who could love me? If my own father won't take time with me, then who can love me? If my own people feel this way about me, then who can love me?"

The question you should consider is not, "What do people think about me?" but "What does God think about me?" To know what God thinks about you, you must read some of what God thinks about you. You'll find it in His Word. What "they" think about you won't determine your destiny—unless you let it.

Even though Jacob, now called Israel, was upset by the dream, the Bible tells us he kept it in mind. He thought about it. He didn't altogether dismiss it. His age and experience with God wouldn't let him completely discount it.

When your children tell you something that God is saying to them, listen and encourage them, even if you don't like the sound of it right away.

During my childhood, God showed me things that He would do in the future. I shared them with my parents, and thank God they listened and encouraged me. I said, "Look, the LORD is showing me preaching to all kinds of people." Thank God they said, "We affirm that. We believe in that.

If God is showing you that, move towards it!" What would've happened if they had rebuked me?

Well, Joseph's brothers went to pasture their father's flock in Shechem, and after a while, Jacob sent Joseph to check on their welfare. When they saw Joseph from a distance, they plotted to kill him. They probably said among themselves, "Here comes that dreamer!" There had already been murder in this generation, and now these boys want to murder their own brother. Family mess!

I wonder how many times we murder our family members with our tongues? "Death and life are in the power of the tongue" (Proverbs 18:21a). When you're not with them, do you murder their influence, authority, and character with your tongue?

But Reuben heard the brothers plotting Joseph's murder and rescued him. Reuben told them to not kill Joseph, but to throw him into a pit. Reuben planned to pull Joseph out of the pit later and return him to his father.

When God is on our side, He orders our steps and protects us from danger—seen and unseen. When God is on our side, He makes even our enemies to be at peace with us!

The other brothers pounced on Joseph when he reached them. They stripped him of his special coat and threw him in an empty cistern. But here's where Reuben's plan went wrong. As the brothers sat down to eat, they saw a caravan of Ishmaelites on their way to Egypt. Judah said to his brothers, "Let's not kill him. He's our own flesh and blood, after all. No, let's sell him."

The other brothers thought it was a good idea, so they pulled Joseph out of the pit and sold him into slavery for twenty pieces of silver. They sold their own brother into slavery, and those traders took Joseph to Egypt. Family mess!

Evidently, Reuben was away from the camp when this happened. When he returned, he went to the pit, only to discover that Joseph wasn't there. He tore his clothes, as a sign of grief and mourning. When he went to his brothers, they came up with the plan of what to tell their father.

Then they took Joseph's special coat, killed a male goat, dipped the coat in the blood and showed it to Jacob. They asked Jacob to identify the coat, and of course he identified it as Joseph's and assumed that his son had been killed. This turn of events sent Jacob into deep grief and mourning, but none of the brothers ever felt sorry enough for their father to tell him what had happened! Codependency, dysfunctionality, family sin, and family mess!

I see families all around me who could relieve the suffering of a family member with just a word—but no one will do it. Just one word of caution would make the difference. Just one word of mercy, one "here's what happened to me or you," one word of encouragement, one word about what happened that dark night thirty years ago, but nobody will say a word.

Meanwhile, in Egypt, Joseph was sold to Potiphar, the captain of the Pharaoh's bodyguards.

Family mess runs all through the roots of this family from Abraham to Isaac to Jacob, and especially through Jacob's sons. No doubt Jacob could see the struggle among his boys. I can imagine him sighing and, saying, "Oh, all my children!" But because Jacob didn't completely dismiss what Joseph had said about his dreams, we get a tip-off that God is at work, in spite of, behind, beneath, through, above, and beyond all of this family mess. God is not through with Joseph yet.

Examine your history. Check out your roots. Find out what happened in your family that nobody wants to talk about. Whatever it is, it's probably still impacting you to-day. Sweeping family mess under the rug doesn't get rid of it. It just hides it until it starts to stink even more. Ignoring the roots of family mess and chopping off the fruit or symptoms doesn't get rid of it. It'll simply sprout up in another place.

Uncover the family mess in your family and put it in the hands of Jesus, knowing that if God sends you to Egypt it's because He's working out His promise, prophecy, and destiny in your life.

Sooner or later, every one of us will be sent down into Egypt where our family members seem to forsake us and everyone around us says, "You're no good," and they sell us out.

When that happens to you, recognize that if God sends you to Egypt, He has a reason for doing so. If God sends you to Egypt, it's because He has a destiny for you down in Egypt and He has to get you there somehow. Therefore, no matter what I go through and no matter what I say, I have a destiny that I know I shall fulfill. I have a destiny, and it is in Jesus Christ.

I've got a destiny and it is in God's Hands. Satan may want to thwart it. He may want to tear it up and depress me, but I recognize on my way down to Egypt that there is a destiny for me. I recognize down in Paddan-Aram that there is a destiny for me. I recognized when they threw me back in prison that it ain't over until God says it is over. The saying is "It ain't over until the fat lady sings!" It has nothing to do with a fat lady singing, but it has a lot to do with a whole lot of Christians praising God. It's not over until God says it is over. And God isn't going to say it is over until He brings you to where He wants you to be.

Family mess can't thwart the destiny of God. Hatred can't thwart the destiny of God. Sexual abuse can't thwart the destiny of God. Neglect can't thwart the destiny of God. Depression can't stop what God wants to do in your life. Praise God!

Discussion Questions

1. Explain dysfunctionality and codependency in your own words.

2. On the continuum of dysfunctionality, where do you consider your own family?

3. If you have children or siblings, can you relate to Joseph? If you don't have children or siblings, have you experienced rivalry with some other person?

4. If you can relate to Joseph's Egypt experience, please share from that perspective.

5. How are your family roots still impacting you?

---

1. John Friel and Linda Friel, *Adult Children: the Secrets of Dysfunctional Families,* Health Communications, Inc., Deerfield Beach, Florida, 1988, pp. 155–156.

2. Robert Homfolt, Frank Minirith and Paul Meier, *Love Is a Choice,* Thomas Nelson Publishers, Nashville, Tennessee, 1989, p. 11.

3. John Friel and Linda Friel, *Adult Children: the Secrets of Dysfunctional Families,* Health Communications, Inc., Deerfield Beach, Florida, 1988, p. 157.

4. Ibid, pp. 74–75.

Chapter Twelve

God Is Greater Than Family Mess
(The Bold and the Beautiful)

Family mess pervades Abraham's family down to the fourth generation. Jacob's children had it in full measure. Yet God's promise to Abraham persists through the fourth generation, all the way to the birth of Jesus Christ.

Let's look at Jacob's son, Judah. He had illicit sex with a Canaanite woman, and produced two illegitimate children. He showed a lack of integrity toward his daughter-in-law, Tamar, when he reneged on his promise to give her to one of his sons. Then he had sex with someone he thought was a prostitute, but who was Tamar. She tricked him, because he broke his word. Family mess!

Despite these shortcomings, when Jacob gave his final prophecy and blessing to his sons, he gave a tremendous blessing to Judah:

> The scepter shall not depart from Judah, nor the ruler's staff from between his feet, until Shiloh comes, and to him shall be the obedience of the peoples. (Genesis 49:10)

Shiloh is a proper name, generally considered by Christian scholars to be a messianic designation of Jesus Christ. Therefore, Jacob prophesied that Judah's destiny was to be a forefather of Jesus Christ.

In the last chapter, we saw Jacob's sons kidnap their own brother, Joseph, with the intent to murder him. By the divine providence of God, they were thwarted, and instead sold him into slavery to Potiphar, captain of Pharaoh's bodyguards.

- Is this the end of the story?
- Will God's promises end with the fourth generation of Abraham dying in slavery?
- Will family mess win out in the end?

Sounds like a *Batman* episode, doesn't it?

- What will happen to the Caped Crusaders?
- Will Batman and Robin be stumped by the Riddler?
- Is this the end of the Dynamic Duo?

I am glad that I can emphatically answer *no!* Throughout this book we've seen God working beneath, behind, through, in spite of, above, and beyond family mess. So we know He will work out this situation. But how?

The Bible tells us "The LORD was with Joseph, so he became a successful man" (Genesis 39:2a). Potiphar saw how the LORD caused everything that Joseph did to prosper. Note that God's blessings were upon Joseph, even though his legacy of family mess was prominent and lengthy.

Is the LORD with you? If He is, He'll make you successful—according to His definition of success. I've seen this happen: Someone with a legacy of family mess will overcome it by the grace and power of Jesus Christ. By every right, this person should be in prison, on drugs, or dead, but God made him or her successful. Oh, the marvelous grace of God!

Potiphar put Joseph in charge of everything in his house, and the LORD blessed Potiphar's house because of Joseph. With Joseph in charge, Potiphar didn't concern himself with anything in his house. We've seen in this book that God blesses others because of those who have found grace in His sight. We've seen that not only the consequences but the *blessings* of a family are transmitted to later generations. But more importantly, God blessed Joseph and all that he did—in spite of his family mess!

God will bless you in spite of your family mess, too. Family mess cannot thwart your destiny when you trust and obey God.

The Bible provides an editorial comment to set the stage for what's to follow. It says that Joseph was handsome in form and in appearance (Genesis 39:6). He had a nice looking body and face. Joseph was truly one of "The Bold and the Beautiful." And it got him in trouble.

"It came about after these events that his master's wife looked with desire at Joseph, and she said, 'Lie with me'" (Genesis 39:7). Potiphar's wife was lusting for sex with Joseph. She didn't say, "I think we can get together." She didn't say, "I like you; do you like me?" She said, "Lie with me." She only wanted sex. That's kind of how things are today, isn't it? People are looking for sex, not love. She didn't love him; he was merely the object of her lust.

I've seen this phenomenon many times. Men who are blessed by God carry an anointing of the Holy Spirit. They stand out, and this anointing sometimes attracts certain women. Driven by the attraction, it seems that these women want to capture the anointing, authority, or power of the anointing in that man. But they don't understand that if they capture it (outside of the will of God, that is), they will ruin it. Delilah tried to capture the anointing that drew her to Samson, but she ruined it instead. In the language of children's stories, it's like killing the goose that laid the golden eggs.

Joseph's response to Potiphar's wife is an example of great integrity:

> But he refused and said to his master's wife, "Behold, with me here, my master does not concern himself with anything in the house, and he has put all that he owns in my charge. There is no one greater in this house than I, and he has withheld nothing from me except you, because you are his wife. How then could I do this great evil and sin against God?" As she spoke to Joseph day after day, he did not listen to her to lie beside her or be with her. (Genesis 39:8–10)

He refused, because of the evil he would perpetrate against God and his master's trust. Joseph's refusal illustrates two things that will greatly reduce adultery or make it largely disappear: care for one's fellow man and care for God.

Now I'm sure Potiphar's wife worked this situation. She probably told him that no one had to know, and that there was no one around. She likely reminded him that he wasn't married and therefore wouldn't be cheating on his wife. But, Joseph was a man of integrity, so he refused her.

Does that surprise you? When you look at Joseph's family history, you may wonder where this integrity came from. It didn't seem to come from Abraham—he was a liar. Neither did he seem to get it from Isaac—he was passive. He didn't get it from Jacob—he was a cheater from his mother's womb. He probably didn't get it from his brothers: they were all messed up. So where did he get it? It must've come from God's dream and Joseph's walk with God.

People often tell me, "The reason I am where I am is because of my mother's nursing habits," or "The reason I am where I am is because somebody didn't do something for me when I was growing up." That's no excuse for not doing the right thing. Joseph chose the path of integrity *in spite of* his family mess.

Have you been offered a tempting proposition? I have. How did you respond? How *are* you responding? You may believe that you can't resist the temptation, but you can. Walk with God and claim your integrity from the dream and destiny that God has given you!

Potiphar's wife didn't stop there. Joseph's rejection only made her want him more, and she pursued him day after day. Satan is persistent! He will continually proposition you. I don't understand how Christians can act like something's wrong, when Satan's attacks them. Get used to it: He's coming back every day. The Bible says that when Jesus was driven by the Holy Spirit into the wilderness Satan left Him—to return at an opportune time (Luke 4:13). Satan is always waiting and lurking. He will be after you everyday.

Joseph once went into the house to do some work and found himself alone with Potiphar's wife (she had probably arranged it that way). This time she grabbed his robe and said, "Lie with me!"

- Joseph didn't try to think his way out of the situation.
- He didn't reason with her.
- He didn't pray about the situation.
- He didn't rebuke the devil.
- He *ran* and left his garment in her hand.

The first, best response to temptation is a good pair of tennis shoes and a burst of energy. This is no time to get spiritual: "Oh, I'm praying about this. I'm praying about you!" Prayer won't immediately help you in some situations. You've got to run and not give the devil opportunity.

This infuriated Potiphar's wife, so she accused him of attempted rape. She broadcast her accusations to the men of her household. You can see there was no love here, only lust. Love wants what's best for the other person, even at its own expense. Lust wants what it wants, when it wants it, even at the expense of the other person.

When Potiphar heard his wife's accusations, his anger burned. He believed his trust in Joseph had been repaid with treachery. So he threw Joseph into jail.

- What's going on?
- What's going to happen to Joseph's dream?
- Why would God allow this to happen?

It looked bad for Joseph, even though he'd done the right thing. He was caught up in someone else's family mess. Nevertheless, by now you know that if God has a destiny for you, it will come to pass. God would allow Joseph to go to prison to work out His plan. As long as Joseph was Potiphar's servant, he couldn't be second in command of Egypt.

Sometimes God will allow you to experience a personal prison to work out His plan in your life. This is often when many of us lose faith, become bitter, and let our confusion rob us of God's blessings. We think, "If God loves me, why is this painful thing happening?"

But Joseph doesn't seem to have responded negatively. He simply continued to serve God in a new place. That's amazing to me.

The same thing happened to Joseph in prison that had happened to him in Potiphar's house: God began to prosper everything he did, so the chief jailer put everything in the whole jail under Joseph's supervision, and the LORD prospered everything that Joseph did.

God will work beneath, behind, through, above, and beyond family mess. He will bless you no matter where you are when you trust in Him, His dream, and His destiny for your life.

It was in prison that Joseph met Pharaoh's former cupbearer and baker, who were once influential people in Egypt. God sometimes sends us to strange places to make important contacts. One night the cupbearer and the baker both had a dream. When Joseph saw them in the morning, he noticed they were dejected, so he asked them what was wrong.

The cupbearer told Joseph his dream and Joseph, by the power of God, interpreted it. He told the cupbearer that in three days Pharaoh would restore him to his post. Joseph asked the cupbearer to remember him in prison, after his restoration.

I believe Joseph tried to manipulate his situation to his advantage. He used human means to try to effect God's plan. Of course it didn't work, but he tried anyway. Perhaps we're seeing a little of his father, Jacob the cheater, seeping through.

When the baker saw that the cupbearer's interpretation was favorable, he told Joseph his dream. So, Joseph also interpreted his dream, but the interpretation was unfavorable.

He told him that in three days he would have his head cut off.

In three days, both dreams were fulfilled exactly as Joseph had interpreted them. It was Pharaoh's birthday. He had a feast for all his servants and he restored the cupbearer to the palace. But the baker was beheaded.

Now, in those days, the cupbearer was the royal food-taster. His job was to be sure that no one would try to poison the king. He was sometimes an adviser and often in the presence of the king. But this man didn't remember Joseph's request. Try as he might, Joseph couldn't manipulate God's plan and timing, because God is sovereign.

Nor can you manipulate God's plan and time. God is Sovereign! Therefore, you can't fix it, turn it around, or make God do what you want Him to do. God is sovereign! He has you where He wants you, because this is where He wants to work some things out. I often hear people say; "I just think that I would be all right if I had another husband. I know He can work with this one, but . . ." But, you can't fix that. That's in God's hands. He'll work it out the way He wants to work it out. So, you might as well leave it alone.

After two more years, Pharaoh had a dream. It was only when no one could interpret the dream that the cupbearer remembered Joseph and told Pharaoh about him. Pharaoh sent for Joseph, and he interpreted the dream. Consequently, Pharaoh elevated him to the second highest position in the land—second only to himself.

- Joseph—descendant of Jacob the trickster, Isaac the passive well-digger, and Abraham the reluctant father of faith—was now elevated by God to the second most powerful position in the world.

- Joseph—the favorite son of his father, the one who was hated by his brothers and sold into slavery—was elevated by God to the second most powerful position in the world.

- Joseph—who came from a family laden with family mess—was now elevated by God to the second most powerful position in the world. He became one of the greatest rulers of all time.

Little did Joseph's brothers know when they plotted to kill him and sell him into slavery that they were sending him on his way to God's dream and destiny! Little do our relatives or church family know that when they plot to kill us with their mouths and when they sell us into slavery that they're sending us on our way to our destiny in Jesus Christ.

God has a dream, a destiny, and a plan for your life. If you trust in God, even family mess can't stop it, because God works beneath, behind, through, in spite of, above, and beyond family mess. *God is greater than family mess!*

I want to look at two Scriptures that sum up God's work in spite of family mess in Joseph's life.

> Now before the year of famine came, two sons were born to Joseph, whom Asenath, the daughter of Potiphera priest of On, bore to him. Joseph named the firstborn Manasseh, "For," he said, "God has made me forget all my trouble and all my father's household." He named the second Ephraim, "For," he said, "God has made me fruitful in the land of my affliction." (Genesis 41:50–52)

There are some important lessons for us here:

- *God can make you forget about all your trouble.* He can make you forget about everything that happened in your past. That should excite you.

- *God can make you forget your father's entire dysfunctional household.* This doesn't mean that Joseph didn't have to deal with them anymore. Jehovah God sent all of his brothers to him, down in Egypt. It means that God can make you forget about them, so they aren't the predominant, preoccupying, negative force in your life.

- *God can make you fruitful in the land of your affliction.* God made Joseph fruitful in the land of his affliction, i.e., Egypt. He did the same thing with Jesus. People looked at Jesus and said, "Can anything good come out of Nazareth? Don't we know His mother? Isn't His mother's name Mary? Isn't His father named Joseph? I used to work with Joseph, down in the carpentry business. I know them. Nothing good can come out of there." But God said, "I'll take this boy and make something out of Him and lift Him up. I don't care what the world says about it, or how they look at Him." And God can make something out of you. Praise God!

The second Scripture is a favorite of Bible readers. It's Joseph's response to his brothers after the death of their father. They wanted to know if Joseph was now going to seek vengeance for everything they'd done to him.

> But Joseph said to them, "Do not be afraid, for am I in God's place? As for you, you meant evil against me, but God meant it for good in order to bring about this present result, to preserve many people alive." (Genesis 50:19–20)

Beloved, never usurp the place of God. "Vengeance is mine," says the LORD, "I will repay" (see Romans 12:19). God will take care of the hatred, cruelty, and mistreatment of your family. He will take the evil they work against you and work it to your good.

Have you experienced this? Someone will go behind your back to smear you, but when all is said and done they're the ones who are smeared. God takes what they said and turns it around and sends it another way to work out His plans for you. There's no weapon formed against you that can ultimately prosper, when you are in God's will. "God causes all things to work together for good to those who love God, to those who are called according to His purpose" (Romans 8:28).

And finally, God will bring about His dream and destiny for you through the family mess that He allows in your life. He will use family mess as a vehicle to put you in a place to preserve many people! God wants to take whatever has happened to you and turn it into a ministry.

Maybe you've been raped. That's a horrible, horrible thing, but God will take that rape and turn it into a ministry, so that you can help others who have gone through the same thing.

Maybe you've been abused. That's a horrible thing, but God will take the abuse and bless you and comfort you, and have you minister to others who have been abused.

God will take your divorce and, after you've been all messed up for five or six years, He'll heal you, comfort you, and give you a ministry dealing with other divorced people.

God will take you when you're full of anger and He'll rid you of that anger, turn you around, and give you a ministry comforting others with a comfort wherewith you yourself have been comforted. He'll take the evil that people do to you and turn it around.

Hear it one last time: God works beneath, behind, in spite of, through, above, and beyond family mess to bring you to your destiny. God is greater than family mess!

Discussion Questions

1. In what ways do you see God working beneath, behind, above, and beyond your family mess?

2. What is your spiritual dream?

3. How do you think God will fulfill your dream through your own personal family mess?

4. Share one of your difficult experiences that you believe will lead you towards God's ultimate dream and destiny.

5. In what personal way do you see God being greater than your family mess?

Conclusion

Thanks for taking this Bible journey with me! We've traveled through valleys and over mountains. We've faced dangers and seen the providence of Almighty God. We've seen Abraham leave home under the direction of Jehovah God, not knowing where he was going to go, but God guided him from the legacy of Babylonia to the legacy of the Promised Land.. We explored the family mess between Sarah and Hagar, Isaac and Jacob, and Abraham and Sarah.

We've followed this family's mess through the twelve sons of Jacob. There were many low points and valleys in this family. But, we persisted and saw Joseph rise out of the valley of family mess to the pinnacle of world leadership through the grace, providence, and blessings of Jehovah God.

On this journey, we've learned that God is greater than family mess. God worked through, beneath, behind, above, beyond, and in spite of family mess to deliver Joseph to the mountaintop of his destiny. Neither Terah's idolatry, nor Abraham's passivity, nor Isaac's lies about his wife, nor

Jacob's tricks, nor the treachery of Jacob's sons could keep God from lifting Joseph above this mess. Joseph was the one, through the grace and power of God, who broke the chain of family mess in his family.

You can be the one who breaks it in your family.

Soap operas never end, but this one ends in the way that life will end for all of us who trust God to walk with us through family mess: "And they lived happily ever after." Remember, God is greater than family mess!

To order additional copies of

GOD IS GREATER THAN...

Have your credit card ready and call

Toll free: (877) 421-READ (7323)

or send $12.99* each plus $5.95 S&H**

to
**WinePress Publishing
PO Box 428
Enumclaw, WA 98022**

or order online at:
www.winepresspub.com

*Washington residents please add 8.4% tax.
**Add $1.50 S&H for each additional book ordered.

Please visit The House of the Lord
web site: www.thotl.org